Calcutta Poor

Calcutta Poor

Elegies on a City above Pretense

— Frederic C. Thomas

 An East Gate Book

M. E. Sharpe
Armonk, New York
London, England

An East Gate Book

All photographs by Frederic C. Thomas

Library of Congress Cataloging-in-Publication Data

Thomas, Frederic C.
Calcutta poor : elegies on a city above pretense / Frederic C. Thomas.
p.   cm.
"An East Gate book."
Includes bibliographical references.
ISBN 1-56324-981-2 (hard).
1. Poor—India—Calcutta.
2. Economic assistance, Domestic—India—Calcutta.
I. Title
HV4140.C34T45   1996
362.5′0954′147—dc20
96-35877
CIP

Printed in the United States of America

The paper used in this publication meets the minimum requirements of the
American National Standard for Information Sciences—
Permanence of Paper for Printed Library Materials,
ANSI Z 39.48-1984.

BM (c)   10   9   8   7   6   5   4   3   2   1

Contents

Preface

With growing numbers of poor in their cities, developing countries face increasing difficulty in offering living standards consistent with the expectations of modern life. In this regard Calcutta is often seen as the classic case of urban failure. The city is notorious for its poverty—perhaps unfairly so. Its sidewalk dwellers, street children, and scavengers have become a cliché for the worst in human degradation. Meanwhile, comparatively little attention has been paid to Calcutta's experience in addressing the needs of its poorest citizens.

Both a historical and an anthropological perspective are needed. Present-day conditions must be seen against the backdrop of the city's history. Neighborhood studies focusing on the immediate context in which people live are essential, of course. But the lessons that emerge from these studies are rarely heeded by politicians and planners attuned to different agendas and city-wide solutions. The observations tend to be too anecdotal and relativistic to be of much practical use, unless placed in a broader policy framework. Also, such studies are often frozen in time, so that little is known of the dynamics of poverty and what the future will be like. To do more than simply enrich the senses, ethnographies must reach theoretical conclusions while at the same time not blotting out the rich detail of everyday life. Otherwise, there is the risk, as in many theoretical studies, that poverty becomes an abstraction, and the recalcitrant facts and ambiguities that are exposed at the neighborhood level are left largely unexplained.

This study attempts to bridge this gap. It is not about the urban development of Calcutta, on which there is already a vast body of literature. Nor is it an in-depth study of a particular slum for the purpose of extrapolating experience which might have more general application and provide broad insights and lessons. The diversity of Calcutta's population (castes, creeds, natives, and migrants) and the variety of slum environments (multistory tenements, bustees, refugee colonies, squatter settlements, sidewalks) would limit the value of any attempt at generalization on the basis of a particular slum.

This study describes the living and working conditions of Calcutta's poor in an effort to get beyond generalities and better understand the practical realities of impoverishment. It draws heavily on investigations done by others. In dealing with its poverty, Calcutta has had a long experience which should be looked at critically to determine the extent to which solutions are possible and, conversely, the extent to which certain forms of poverty may be perversely immune to treatment.

To do this, I have reviewed much of the literature, including many unpublished papers. On several occasions since the late 1970s I have made one- and two-month visits to Calcutta and have met with municipal officials, representatives of charitable organizations, researchers, businessmen, and bustee leaders. To acquire a street-level perspective and avoid overly theoretical speculation, I have spent many hours walking through different slums, observing activities taking place in the labyrinth of alleys and courtyards and talking informally to the people I met. A rudimentary command of Bengali was of great help in establishing contact and in validating the sincerity of my interest. This study, in short, stems more from a pleasurable and spontaneous process of confirming and supplementing the oral and written observations of others than from any rigorous process of participant observation or structured interviews.

Acknowledgments

My investigations would not have been possible without the valuable help I received from many persons in Calcutta. I am especially indebted to Sudhendu Mukherjee, who first introduced me to the bustees in 1978 and inspired me to pursue the subject further. I also want to thank those who shared with me their valuable insights and experience in dealing with Calcutta's poor and provided me with personal papers and studies which would not have been otherwise available. In this respect, I should particularly mention Mohammed Alamgir, Nirmala Banerjee, Tapan Banerjee, Mohit Bhattacharya, Bimalesh Bhattacharya, A.N. Bose, Eliana Chaudhuri, Samir Chaudhuri, Ashin Das, Prabhat R. Das, Abhijit Dasgupta, Biplad Dasgupta, Leslie Green, Animesh Halder, Vijay Jagannathan, Purnendu Jha, Raj M. Kapoor, M.S. Maitra, Rabial Mallick, Bijli Mallik, Braz Menezes, Madhu Mishra, Shourabh Mukerji, D.K. Roy, Kalyan Roy, Subhankar Roy, Asok Sen, Jai Sen, and K.C. Sivaramakrishnan. For her kindness and endless patience in teaching me Bengali, I express my sincere gratitude to Aditi Sen.

I am happy to acknowledge the grant support provided by the Richard Lounsbery Foundation in New York and particularly wish to thank its late President, Alan F. McHenry. My thanks go also to the Society for Applied Anthropology, which sponsored my research, and to the American Institute for Indian Studies, which facilitated my work in Calcutta and helped me obtain official approval from the Government of India. I am most appreciative to the Center for South Asian Studies for their cooperation in providing access to the library facilities of the University of California, Berkeley.

Calcutta Poor ～

Introduction

Almost every book written about Calcutta begins with extravagant language describing the city's squalor and putrefaction. It is as though Calcutta has always had a perverse fascination as a dreadful place. As early as the 1770s, the first Governor of Bengal, Robert Clive, called it "the most wicked place in the universe." Nearly one hundred years later, one of his successors, Sir George Trevelyan, wrote: "Find, if you can a more uninviting spot than Calcutta. . . . The place is so bad by nature that human efforts could do little to make it worse, but that little has been done faithfully and assiduously." Rudyard Kipling in his oft-quoted portrayal, called Calcutta "the city of dreadful night—a city of unspeakable poverty, of famine, riot and disease . . . where the cholera, the cyclone, the crow come and go, by the sewerage rendered fetid, by the sewer made impure." Young Winston Churchill was more matter-of-fact and whimsical when he wrote to his mother: "I shall always be glad to have seen it—for the same reason Papa gave for being glad to have seen Lisbon—namely, that it will be unnecessary for me ever to see it again." Mark Twain, who stayed only one or two days, found the weather "enough to make the brass doorknob mushy." On a visit in 1963, V.S. Naipaul could only conclude that Calcutta was "an abomination."

In his review of Harold Lubell's 1974 book on Calcutta's economy and employment structure, Norton Ginsburg of the University of Chicago wrote:

> How many times has that great, sprawling, simmering metropolis been written off as a model of what a proper city ought not to be—teeming, disease ridden, seething with frustration and ethnic and religious hatred, poverty stricken, a colonial anomaly, and hot, my god, so hot. . . . Even in India, Calcutta has an image problem, and its press, at least to the outside world—and that means just about everywhere beyond Bengal—has been abominable.[1]

There is no denying, though, that this historic city may be among the more unpleasant environments on the face of the earth: the masses of people, the choking pollution, the clogged drains, the cramped bustees and crumbling mansions, the jumble of carts, the beggars and crippled children, the fetid piles of refuse being picked over by emaciated mothers in soiled saris, flea-bitten pariah dogs, and wildly cawing crows. Scenes like this have made Calcutta into a cliché of squalor and despair. Yet clichés can often be misleading. There are other cities which are as bad if not worse. A higher percentage of Bombay's population lives in slums more horrendous than one finds in Calcutta, and many of Calcutta's notorious bustees have been improved with drains, sanitary facilities, and other amenities.

Besides, there is nothing moribund about Calcutta. It is a vigorous and vibrant city, politically the liveliest city in India. Its rich intellectual life cannot be ignored. Cultural activities go on in the same streets which are haunted by poverty. "In fact, one feels that there is a connection between the bad drains, dead puppies, crippled children and heated discussions on Ezra Pound, Elliot or Gramsci, or a musical evening with Nikhil Banerjee [the famous Calcutta musician and associate of Ravi Shankar]."[2]

What is it about Calcutta's poverty that attracts journalists, filmmakers, travel writers and curious visitors? Young volunteers from abroad working with the poor were asked this question. An Irish nun serving with Mother Teresa spoke of the "beauty of the poor." Could it be said that she was romanticizing pitiful conditions or equating poverty with moral rectitude? Along the same lines, another volunteer said that the poor were here "to keep us compassionate," as if they exist, poor souls, for our own uplift and benefit. Their deplorable circumstances serve to remind us of our guilt and compel us to show concern. "We in the West have profited from the third world—our debt then takes the form of intervening in the system that keeps the poor poor," as another volunteer put it.

The tenor of their replies is revealing, particularly in turning their experience in confronting poverty back upon themselves. Calcutta's poverty has become virtually a tourist attraction. The initial impact of scenes of human degradation on the sensitivities of the visitor soon wear off, however. "If you stay just two days, it's horrid, if you stay longer you get to love it." Strange routines and recognitions, even the most repellent and shocking, become familiar after more exposure. The flies and the stench become part of the scene. But at the same time, fortunately, a feeling of uncertainty and humility takes hold: "The longer you stay here the more you realize that you hardly know the place at all." And mixed with these reactions is the joy of discovery: "Images crowd in, impress themselves, force thought, and I have to find its expression in myself." Or as another person said: "You come here not so much to find yourself as to lose yourself."[3]

Summarizing these answers to the question of why they were working among the most poverty-stricken of Calcutta's population does not do justice to the seriousness of the thoughts behind them. They can only suggest what it is that attracts visitors—like flies to festering sores? Not so much, it seems, to study and better appreciate the conditions or to resolve the problems, but for more personal reasons. The reactions of the volunteers were largely introspective: a mix of guilt, self-fulfillment, self-discovery, self-awareness, a questioning of one's own values rather than an understanding of Indian values. Poverty was being treated as an

abstraction that had primary importance in enhancing the sensitivities of the observer.

Commenting on these reactions, an Indian writer observed that
what went unnoticed in their exclusive involvement with gross
poverty was all the work that was being done by Indians to
improve conditions. Consequently, outsiders tend to see poverty
as a permanent condition and the poor as a category which will
always stay that way.[4] Perhaps a valid point; perhaps not. The
extent to which poverty is intractable whatever efforts may be
undertaken to deal with it, is what this book is about.

There was public furor over the filming of some sequences of
City of Joy, the name given by Dominique Lapierre to Pilkhana,
the huge slum described in his book. By and large, it was a
sympathetic account. He admired the spirit and resilience of
those slum dwellers he got to know. It seems ironic, therefore,
that his sensitive narrative regarding the deplorable conditions
was burned by the very people he wrote about.

When later filming the story, Roland Joffé, the director, in-
curred the wrath of Calcuttans for daring to show the seamy side
of the city. Even though the film script had been officially
cleared, the film unit, working in Calcutta in early 1992, faced
demonstrations in front of the hotel where it was staying and
large, unruly crowds at filming locations in the slums. According
to an Indian UN official, Indian intellectuals believed that, with
the film, "Calcutta will become the favourite pin-up of the por-
nographers of poverty. Westerners are going to munch popcorn
in air-conditioned theatres as they stare at flickering images of
dying Indian babies. This is a new kind of voyeurism, which has
no interest in the totality of Calcuttan reality. . . ." The official
went on, however, to argue for the right to make such a film and
the value it could have. It would make people in the West aware
of the problems Indians were struggling with dignity and selfless-
ness to overcome.[5]

This is what makes Calcutta especially worth study: how it is
dealing with these problems. In the late sixties, the need to take

drastic action was presented in terms verging on the apocalyptic by an international panel:

> We have not seen human degradation on a comparable scale in any other city in the world. This is a matter of one of the greatest urban concentrations in existence rapidly approaching the point of breakdown in terms of its economy, housing, sanitation, transport and the essential amenities of life. . . . If the final breakdown is to take place, it would be a disaster for mankind of a more sinister sort than any disaster of flood or famine. It would be confession of failure, at the first major confrontation, of mankind's ability to organise the vast, rapidly growing urban concentrations into which humanity seems inevitably destined to move.[6]

Much has been accomplished since then in terms of potable water, underground sewage, sanitary facilities, health services, nutrition, and child care, and much of what we now hear and read about Calcutta can be suspected of hyperbole. Conditions are no worse than in many other Third World cities—but the image problem will not go away.

Kipling described Calcutta as a city which is "above pretense," and it is still true, a hundred years later, that Calcuttans seem to accept conditions as they are. They have lower expectations. They see problems as beyond their control. In a perverse way they also love the city. As New Yorkers know, great cities can inspire—and sometimes depress—their inhabitants. So also Calcuttans have an intense love-hate relationship with their city. "We cannot drink the water or breathe the air but would live nowhere else." Inured to the deterioration of their once-splendid city, they treat the degradation almost with indifference. In this respect, the city may be the vision of the future. It may represent the only realistic means of coping in a Third World of exploding populations, environmental degradation, rural–urban migration, massive unemployment and underemployment, and the staggering costs of providing basic urban services.

As cities grow and land fills up, relocating the poor on the fringes where there are few opportunities for employment is no longer an acceptable solution. Inner-city slums become more crowded, and tumbledown squatter shacks fill every nook and cranny and spill out onto the pavements. As the large-scale manufacturing and processing activities that once provided jobs to newcomers lose their importance, people must depend increasingly on petty services, trading, and illicit activities for their livelihoods. Overcrowding and subhuman work conditions place strains on the ties of ethnic origin, creed, and caste that traditionally provided the individual with essential support. These urban trends and the vitality of these ties under conditions of severe deprivation are vividly demonstrated in Calcutta.

Impressions

As the eastern sky begins to lighten, I leave the hotel and walk up the broad Chowringhee. Heavy mist hugs the Maidan, the expanse of parkland in the heart of the city, where some dim figures can be seen in the distance going about their early morning yoga exercises. Under the arcades along the Chowringhee, families are still asleep, like bundles of rags cast randomly about upon the sidewalk. The streets are empty; black and yellow taxis stationed at intersections; clusters of rickshaws at curbside, the rickshaw wallahs doubled up uncomfortably on their narrow seats, asleep. Near the market, men are stretched out on their tilted, two-wheeled barrows, long shafts resting on the pavement.

The first rays of sunlight penetrate into the street and bring each scene into sharp relief. The bundles of rags begin to stir. Bodies emerge, blinking, yawning, sitting up, stretching. Early risers stand about, shivering, wrapped in their shawls. Others gather by the hand pump, filling metal bowls and plastic pails, and begin to wash, soaping vigorously, heads, bodies, and under their lungis. Those who are not fully awake sit squinting into the keen morning sunlight, which offers little warmth, smoking a biri or massaging their teeth with a neem twig. A man reads a newspaper aloud to his companions. Tea shops begin to open, the smoking ghee filters the sunlight. Milky tea is sucked noisily from small clay cups, which are then tossed into the street. Hugging the walls, sidewalk barbers meticulously shave their first customers, who hold up small mirrors to keep an eye on the progress. At a quiet corner, at the base of a tree, a few devotees stand solemnly before a small Hindu shrine whose garlanded image of a special divinity is decorated with quince leaves and sandalwood paste.

The sun gets warmer. Flies crawl on the sleeping dogs and the late risers, still shrouded from head to foot. Early pedestrians take care to step around them. Tea shops and corner stalls are now doing a brisk business selling tea, chappatis, samosas, spiced chickpeas, biri and other cigarettes, betel nut and lime paste or other condiments delicately wrapped in a leaf. The rickshaw and handcart pullers, now fully awake, perch silently on their vehicles waiting for a fare or some cargo, chewing stalks of sugarcane for the energy they will need to face another arduous day. An old woman with matted hair eats breakfast off of a piece of newspaper, a puppy curled in her lap. An entire family in a circle surrounded by their belongings reach into a common bowl. A young couple, lying facing each other on the sidewalk, a baby between them, talk quietly as if in the privacy of a bedroom. Beneath an arcade, articles for sale are being laid out on low wooden platforms; the merchants sit cross-legged in the middle, building up the displays around them: clothing, shoes, sandals, plastic bags, ballpoint pens, flashlight batteries, newspapers, magazines, soap, toothpaste, combs, trinkets, bangles. On a side street, fruit and vegetable vendors carefully stack their produce: pyramids of oranges, small fat bananas, potatoes, open sacks of rice, cauliflower, green coconuts.

By now a growing crescendo: heavy trucks revving up, clattering metal blinds being raised, peddlers calling out their wares. Each activity, each livelihood remains circumscribed and self-contained. Everyone goes about his business, unmindful of the hubbub all around. Women at the pump wash cooking pots and clothes on the curb. Another woman plasters cakes of cow dung mixed with rice straw on the walls to dry as fuel. Men cook deep-fried pastries at a sidewalk restaurant. Clusters of young children pick through discarded embers looking for salvageable pieces of charcoal. A pavement artist, sitting cross-legged, begins his crayon drawings of gods and goddesses. There is no encroachment despite the congestion, the shoppers, the meandering cows, the jostling of pushcarts, the shouting of hawkers, the insistent honking of cars, the whining of three-wheeled motorized rickshaws. Rays of sunlight slice through the exhaust fumes and the smoke of charcoal braziers and dung-burning cooking stoves which cloud the air.

Crows on garbage piles hop once, twice, and take off. Young girls in blue and white uniforms, wearing "Keep Calcutta Clean" buttons, sweep the sidewalks in front of the entrance to their school. There is evident pride in the city. Even under most inauspicious conditions, there is nothing slovenly. Every effort is made to preserve dignity and self-respect: the care given to washing oneself, one's clothes, taxi, bicycle, or rickshaw amid the onslaught of human and motorized traffic pressing in from all sides; the fastidious inspection in the small handheld mirror after the sidewalk barber is done; the spotless white shirts and carefully pressed trousers of young men picking their way through the crowd or lunging for a precarious handhold on the overcrowded bus en route to a low-paying job in some dingy office.

I can walk about without feeling self-conscious and too much of a tourist, observe the private lives being played out on the street, look closely at poverty without embarrassment. People seem oblivious to my presence; they have their own lives to lead. There is a vigorous and structured economy at work here. People are friendly and very alert. There is no badgering or harassment until I am back on the Chowringhee or along Park Street, where the tourist hotels are located. There a women in a ragged sari, holding a baby, rushes forward to ask for bakshish. Men offer to change money or furnish young girls, young boys, marijuana, whatever else might be wanted. Appallingly mutilated specimens

of humanity with unseeing eyes, tin cans clutched between tooth-
less gums, shriveled arms, twisted legs, or no legs at all lie on the
pavement, strategically deposited beside plastic sheets, which are
held down at the four corners by stones and serve to catch a
sprinkling of coins. Have Calcuttans conquered their squeamish-
ness as they walk by, seemingly indifferent to this human misery? Certainly not so in the case of the foreign visitor who passes
quickly along with determined smile and eyes averted; this is the
Calcutta that will be remembered.

A visit to Mother Teresa's home for the dying in Kalighat is
inevitably part of the itinerary. It is a quiet sanctuary next to the
temple of the goddess Kali and its throng of devotees. There are
about forty beds for men and, in a separate dormitory, somewhat
fewer for women; on them shrunken figures, some sitting, some
lying, some sleeping. The overall impression is surprisingly
pleasant, enlivened by children running about; there are "nonformal" classes for street children regularly held upstairs. Young
foreigners work as volunteers. Not told what to do, they manage
somehow to settle in and help: washing bedclothes, feeding the
patients, picking maggots off a dying woman, and then seeing
what else there is to do. They say that the work has more value
for them than for the dying. Besides, caring on this scale can only
have symbolic importance in a megalopolis of almost twelve
million souls, half of whom live in poverty. Perhaps the involvement of expatriates makes the symbol more meaningful.

I need to talk to officials who deal with urban problems. At
their desks beneath a battery of fans in the outer office, clerks
type, read newspapers, talk on telephones, and rest their heads on
their desks. From time to time, a peon is sent out to bring tea and
pass it around. I am always included. Tables are piled with dusty
files held together by pink cloth ribbons. Calendars on the walls
show religious festivals and other holidays prominently in red,
promising release from this drab routine.

The interview finally takes place inside, where several officials are already having a conference, one of them shouting into a
telephone, another calling for a report or ordering tea, while an-

other answers my questions in a loud voice (so that the foreigner will better understand?). What I need are recent progress reports, studies, evaluations, but they are not yet available. The latest information they give me is several years old, but still reputedly reliable—number of beneficiaries, lakh rupees spent, official guidelines, other useful data—abstractions with little feel for what is actually going on. Like that of bureaucrats everywhere, their social consciousness is more theoretical than practical. To talk about poverty in theoretical terms, however, is no substitute for understanding. Still, the subject is handled candidly, without euphemism and pompousness, which is refreshing.

I am impatient to visit a slum. To prepare the way, one of the officials suggests that he accompany me; on my own, the slum dwellers will be suspicious. The next day we meet, as agreed, at the entrance to a *bustee,* as the slums of Calcutta are called. The official arrives by car with the local ward councillor in tow, for protocol reasons, I suppose. Clusters of people watch impassively as we make our way down the narrow lane flanked by drains, past doors opening into small courtyards each surrounded by cubicles in which whole families live. An invitation to come in and look inside one of the courtyards is immediate and genuine. By now, however, our official party has been augmented by the arrival of a young man speaking some English, a self-appointed interlocutor in case of need, plus a gaggle of curious, smiling children. We crowd in, greeting the occupants with palms together, ducking under the lines hung with clothes and stepping carefully around some chickens, a tethered goat, a dog with puppies, some baskets and buckets, a pile of half-burned coal, a stack of dried dung cakes. I look into one of the dark cubicles where there is a handsome woman with a baby on her hip and behind her a bony, unshaven man sitting on the bed, other people indiscernible in the darkness, some shiny aluminum pots and water jugs and other possessions neatly stacked. That so many people can live an ordered day-to-day existence in so little space is hard to believe.

My opening questions seem painfully prosaic and empty: How

many families live in this hutment? Are the families related?
What sort of work do they do? How much rent do they pay?
Does the landlord live in the bustee or not? Who owns the chickens, the goat over there? Do the children go to school? And so
on, unimaginatively, unable under the conditions to shift easily to
some less superficial topic such as bustee politics, communal
violence, or abuse of women. The self-designated interlocutor is
quick with most of the answers even though it turns out that he
does not live in that particular hutment and is not related to the
occupants. The ward councillor occasionally contributes an official answer for my benefit, the foreign visitor assiduously taking
notes. Replies from the residents themselves, who look quietly
on, heads bobbing in agreement, would be more convincing.
Still, they go out of their way to be helpful, to show me everything: the kitchen area, the plugged drain, the disabled pump, the
sick child, the latrine . . . more than I really care to see. To
capture any of it in a photograph is next to impossible. The space
is too confined and, once the camera is out, the children crowd in
close to the lens. I would like to stay longer, for their welcome is
genuine, but my escorts suggest that we should be moving along.

By now it is clear that even a rudimentary understanding of
poverty will come not from a linear process of getting information and facts, of structured interviews and carefully selected
informants, of sticking doggedly to the subject at hand. It will
come instead from a process of accidental driftings, walking
down one lane instead of another, remaining always open to
serendipity, blurred observations, overlapping and conflicting insights, abrupt U-turns in conversation which depend on who happens to enter the room or interject an unsolicited opinion.
Gradually a composite picture which you can count on will
emerge. Some solid basis can also be established from the historical record, a framework at least within which to move forward
and lock in impressions.

Black Town and the City of Palaces

Why, it has been often asked, did Job Charnock, soldier of fortune, choose in 1690 such a place to found a settlement? The site was unhealthy, a low, swampy area, crisscrossed by a tangle of creeks emptying into the Hooghly, the westernmost distributary of the Ganges, and skirted on the east by a vast stretch of saltwater lake. The topography foreordained conditions of pestilence and monsoon flooding that the new town would have to endure. As Kipling wrote:

> Thus the midday halt of Charnock—more's the pity,
>   Grew a city.
> As the fungus sprouts chaotic from its bed,
>   So it spread—
> Chance-directed, chance-erected, laid and built
>   On the silt—
> Palace, byre, hovel—poverty and pride—
>   Side by side;
> And, above the packed and pestilential town,
>   Death looked down.[7]

Palace, byre, hovel—the contrast tersely drawn between the stately dwellings of the governing elite and the fetid slums of Black Town, where the native population lived. The central area around Fort William and the esplanade was called the City of Palaces because of its public buildings and princely residences inhabited by Englishmen. They first came as factors of the East India Company and later as rulers of India.

> The situation of the elegant garden houses, as the villas on the left bank were called, surrounded by verdant grounds laid out in the English style, with the Ganges flowing before them, covered with boats and shipping struck me . . . as singularly beautiful. These charming residences announced our approach [in 1792] to the modern capital of the East, and bespoke the wealth and luxury of its inhabitants. Turning suddenly to the north, at the end of this reach, the "City of Palaces" with its lofty detached flat-roofed mansions and the masts of its innumerable shipping, appeared before us on the left bank of the Ganges, and on the same side, in the foreground of this beautiful perspective, were the extensive ramparts of Fort William.[8]

Radiating out to the north and east in those early years were a labyrinth of thatched huts, malodorous drains, which had not been cleaned since the last rains, and narrow winding lanes swarming with humanity, "where the scavenging carts are the rarest of visitors and the ghostly glimmer of an occasional and inadequate gas lamp furnishes the solitary illumination. Not a thousand yards from Government House, troupes of jackals may be heard after sunset sweeping through the deserted streets and making the night hideous with their fearsome howls." Further out, gardens, fruit trees, and mean huts were clustered in irregular groups around stagnant tanks, amid tufts of bamboo, coconut trees, and plantains, "picturesque and striking to the sight, but extremely offensive to the smell, from the quantity of putrid water, the fumes of wood smoke, coconut oil, and, above all the ghee, which is to the Hindoo his principal luxury."[9]

The journals of British officials, their wives, and visitors out from England portray a life of languid boredom in an unhealthy climate. Foreign residents were attended by a host of cooks, housekeepers, grooms, footmen, torchbearers, watchmen, punkah wallahs (who stirred the torpid air with large, suspended fans), sweepers, and other retainers. But for the sumptuous dinners, the arrival of the steamer from home, horse races, occasional weddings, and all-too-frequent funerals, there was little relief from the torrid indolence of colonial life. The inveterate diarists of that period described in detail the mundane trivia of expatriate lives while devoting little attention to the living conditions and daily activities of the natives, other than some macabre reference to squalor and hopelessness. For the few exceptions who did venture out, the vitality of activity, the sights and sounds of Black Town left a vivid impression:

> The shops are often but six or eight feet square, and seldom twice this size, wholly open in front. . . . Barbers sit in the open street on a mat, and the patient, squatting on his hams, has not only his beard, but part of his head shaved leaving the hair to grow only on his crown. In the tanks and ponds are dobeys [washermen], slapping their clothes with all their might upon a bench or a stone. Little braminy bulls, with their humped shoulders, walk among the crowd, thrusting their noses into the baskets of rice, gram, or peas, with little resistance, except they stay to repeat the mouthful. . . . Palankeens come bustling along, the bearers shouting at the people to clear the way. Peddlers and hucksters utter their ceaseless cries. Religious mendicants with long hair, matted with cow-dung, and with faces and arms smeared with Ganges mud, walk about almost naked, with an air of the utmost impudence and pride, demanding rather than begging gifts. . . . Women crowd about the wells, carrying water on their hips in brass jars. Children run about stark-naked, or with a thin plate of silver or brass, not larger than a tea-cup, hung in front by a cord round the hips. Mud-holes, neglected tanks [reservoirs], decaying carcasses, and stagnant ditches, unite with fumes of garlic, rancid oil, and human filth, to load the air with villainous smells. The *tout-ensemble* of sights, sounds, and smells, is so utterly unlike anything in any other part of the world, that weeks elapse before the sensation of strangeness wears away.[10]

That was in 1839. Except for the palanquins (replaced by horse carriages and later by rickshaws at the beginning of this century), the same vibrancy is as palpable today in some neighborhoods of the city: the bustle of buying and selling, the cows, the pushcarts, the hawkers, the chaos of traffic, the sweating laborers manhandling preposterous loads, the rickshaw pullers jogging barefoot through traffic, the holy men, the children rushing to serve small cups of milky tea, the young executives walking briskly with briefcases, the women gossiping as they pick lice from their children's hair or scrub cooking pots and clothes at the water tap, the line of destitutes with aluminum bowls patiently awaiting their portions of cooked rice from the distribution kiosk of some charity, the circle of men playing cards on the sidewalk, others dozing on charpoys, the beggar stock-still before a small pot in which coins have been placed.

From the earliest days, Black Town was divided into areas based on religion and caste, in one part Hindus, in another Muslims, or the native Portuguese and Armenians. The Hindu areas were then further subdivided into the quarters of the brahmins, scribes, and other occupations, although these distinctions were never too firmly established. The East India Company had allocated its workmen separate quarters in the town and thus the location of different trade guilds: for potters, oil pressers, fishermen, milkmen, palanquin bearers, butchers, dealers in country blankets, sweepers, blacksmiths, washermen, carpenters, weavers, and other vocations. This division by caste left its stamp on the city as it evolved in the late eighteenth and early nineteenth centuries into a more heterogeneous commercial and administrative center.[11]

Black Town was not exclusively given over, however, to the teeming majority living largely in poverty. Situated amid the mud huts and brick tenements were some "handsome houses inclosed in courtyards, belonging to Armenian merchants, Parsees, and Bengalee gentlemen of great wealth and respectability. The avenues which led to these mansions were exceedingly narrow, but the premises themselves were often very extensive, the principal apartment looking out upon pretty gardens. . . ."[12] These residences of prominent families tended to draw clusters of people around them—the artisans and laborers who were needed for service. Calcutta thus became basically a city of huts, the palatial residences of opulent Bengalis surrounded by bazaars and slums.

The houses of the well-to-do were brick-built, two, even three stories high, and flat-roofed. Many of the larger ones consisted of a double quadrangle. They were built in the form of two hollow squares with interior nooks and niches, narrow galleries, and halls for deities. Long verandas, facing inward toward the quadrangle, gave access to the living apartments on the upper floor. This layout provided a room for each married son, and extra rooms, which were kept for visiting daughters and other relatives. The inner section of the house was for the women, who were secluded under purdah, and the children in the daytime. The outer section was for the men, who would conduct their business activities there or pass the hours in conversation or in smoking or playing cards. Many of the older houses had also wooden balconies facing the street.

In sharp contrast, the cottages of Black Town were thatched, with side walls of mud or mats, bamboo, and other combustible materials. Fires were frequent until the middle of the nineteenth century, when the thatched roofs were forbidden by municipal ordinance and converted to tiles. Placed on the bare ground and crammed together without ventilation or drainage, the huts were typically grouped around a tank or pond, which often received most of the domestic refuse and was at the same time used for washing and cooking. Glimpses of the conditions within these slums in the 1880s can be had from the letters which indignant citizens wrote to the editor of Calcutta's principal newspaper:

> Sir, . . . The foul sights and smells are enough to upset the stomach of even a health officer. What with a half-a-dozen large stables, and hovels begrimed with dirt and infested with squalid inhabitants, it is a wonder that some epidemic does not originate here. . . .

Sir, . . . Many of the most important streets have not yet been supplied with any lights at all, to the great inconvenience of people. It is difficult and dangerous to grope one's way in the dark at night. . . .

Sir, . . . The hydrants are few, and situated at too great intervals to adequately supply the wants of a thickly populated locality. All day long they are surrounded by crowds of low-caste people, who in their eagerness to supply themselves with water, frequently fall to fighting, which in many cases results in bloodshed. The better classes send their maid-servants for water, but hustled about by the boisterous crowd, they often as not return with empty vessels. . . .

Sir, . . . a dirty pond, covered with slime and fungus in the middle of hundreds of tiled huts, literally reeking with filth and abomination of sorts, the water of which, I am led to believe, is freely used for washing and culinary purposes. An attempt is being made to fill up the pond with refuse and street sweepings. . . .

Sir, . . . I was not surprised to hear cholera had broken out in the neighbourhood in a virulent form and several people fell victim to it. The sallow, dejected looks of the people who surrounded me told their own tale. Suffering humanity appeals for help. . . .[13]

For much of the eighteenth century, the small English community of traders working for the East India Company lived together in their factories and dined together at their common table. They took on Indian habits in food and dress and frequently married Indian women. They showed respect for Indian authority and curiosity about the native customs and traditions. By the beginning of the nineteenth century, however, the traders had become firmly established in their new role, that of administrators, requiring a new breed of Englishmen with very different attitudes. They discarded "the old habits of the Company 'nabobs' of the previous era—their adoption of native customs like smoking the hubble-bubble, keeping an Indian mistress, and offering *puja* to the goddess Kali at the ancient temple of Kalighat in the south of Calcutta. . . ." Instead, they showed little interest in the local culture and in some instances an extraordinary contempt for the "natives," once described by a Governor-General as "being nearly limited to mere animal functions . . . but with no higher intellect than a dog, an elephant, or a monkey might be supposed to be capable of attaining."[14]

Under the changed conditions, the official community sought to insulate itself from the contamination of the native town. Orders were issued from Fort William banning the entrance of native laborers and vendors into the precincts of the White Town except at certain hours. Prescribed boundaries of ethnic segregation were inevitably transgressed, however. The European could not do without his milkmen, washermen, and domestic servants, who had to live close by. "The miasma from the Crooked Lane or Janbazar, in close proximity to the areas of European exclusiveness, had to be tolerated, and the congestion of China Bazar or Cossitola (areas of both wholesale and retail business attached to the European town) was a necessary evil."[15] Moreover, by the middle of the nineteenth century many of the poorer neighborhoods were occupied by Eurasians and Europeans of lower economic status, making separation along ethnic lines no longer practicable (see map, next page).

By the second half of the nineteenth century, Calcutta had become "the second city of the British empire." With the introduction of railways and the opening of the Suez Canal, its commercial importance increased dramatically. The population more than doubled and property values shot up. The new jute industry began to flourish in Bengal, and quiet river settlements were transformed into noisy centers of industry by the erection of jute mills and the influx of migrant laborers. Recalling the city he had known in his childhood, Rabindranath Tagore, the great poet of Bengal, would write:

> The only thing which gave [the city] a sacred baptism of beauty was the river. I was fortunate enough to be born before the smoke-belching iron dragon had devoured the greater part of the life of its banks; when the landing-stairs descending into its waters, caressed by its tides, appeared to me like the loving arms of the villages clinging to it; when Calcutta . . . had not surrendered body and soul to her wealthy paramour, the spirit of the ledger, bound in dead leather.[16]

In a 1914 plan for rebuilding the city, a line on the map divided Calcutta into two areas of very different character. All that

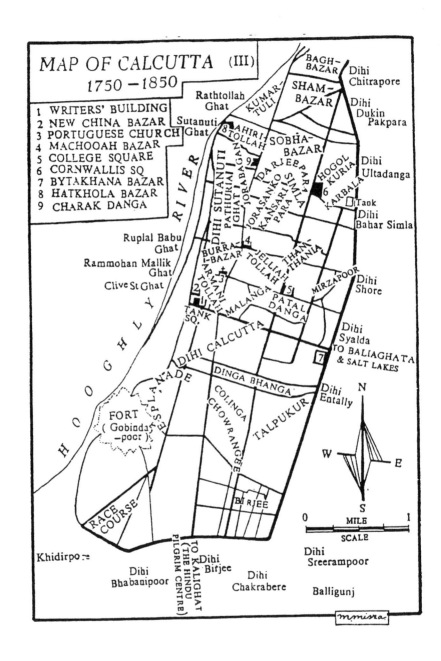

MAP OF CALCUTTA (III)
1750 – 1850

1 WRITERS' BUILDING
2 NEW CHINA BAZAR
3 PORTUGUESE CHURCH
4 MACHOOAH BAZAR
5 COLLEGE SQUARE
6 CORNWALLIS SQ
7 BYTAKHANA BAZAR
8 HATKHOLA BAZAR
9 CHARAK DANGA

lay north and east of the line—Black Town—contained the best and worst of Indian residential quarters and housed the bulk of the population. It included the main Indian markets, the commercial and banking center (Burrabazar), and the old settled neighborhoods (Shyambazar, Jorasanko, Sobhabazar, Paikpara, and Shyampukur), where the wealthiest urban landlords and notables lived. To the south of the line lay the chief business houses of the British, the sterling banks, the seats of government, the public offices, and the leading hotels, and below that, the special residential quarters of European businessmen and administrators and the clubs for cricket, horseback riding, and other diversions.

No line on a map, however, could restrain the pervasive encroachment of poverty and decay. Areas that had contained elegant European residences in extensive grounds began to deteriorate with the establishment of the municipal slaughterhouse and the pumping station for the drainage works. With time, upper- and middle-class neighborhoods became infested by slums. The earlier distinction between the City of Places and Black Town gave way to the Calcutta of today, with slum pockets, known as bustees, in every ward of the city.

Bhadralok and
the Genteel Poor

The Bengali Hindus were first in residence in Calcutta. As interpreters, brokers to the English traders, and go-betweens in judicial and revenue administration, they mediated between the British and the "natives" in economic and administrative matters. Acting as "head bookkeeper, head secretary, supplier of cash, and keeper of secrets," they hired the "under-clerks, door-keepers, stewards, bearers of the silver, slaves, running footmen, torch and branch light carriers, and palanquin-bearers for whose honesty they were answerable."[17] Many of them acquired great influence and wealth. They were known as *babus,* a title of respect in those days reserved for English-speaking Hindus. They entertained lavishly on such occasions as wedding ceremonies or religious festivals, organizing dance performances and elaborate dinner parties, which the Europeans enjoyed.

Their descendants pursued the learned professions and careers in the civil service, in addition to their real estate interests. These well-established, upper- and middle-class extended families formed the *bhadralok*—gentlefolk or respectable people—a social status which embraced landed gentry as well as administrative employees and professions. Although many of them came from the three upper castes of Hindu society—Brahmins (priests scholars), Kayasthas (warrior landowners), and Baidyas (businessmen)—membership was open to all caste groups. Those who acquired status through English education or administrative service and shared a common lifestyle were included. Even men of humble origin, such as small traders, petty administrators, and small landholders, who made money working as junior partners of the English officers and free merchants, could rise in social status in the course of a few generations. And so also, impecuniousness would not automatically deprive a family of its bhadralok standing. The hallmarks of their status were a liberal and secular outlook, a singular attachment to education, and a preference for white-collar jobs. They were distinguished by their behavior, dress, eating habits, and associations. They resided in *pucca*—brick-built—houses, which they either owned or rented, and took pride in their knowledge of the English language and of English manners, which they assiduously emulated. Among them, caste was not given much emphasis. They saw to it that their children married into families of appropriate caste but "avoided a mingling of caste and genealogical concerns with new preoccupations, literary, intellectual, educational and political."[18]

Not included among the bhadralok were the Muslim petty merchants, artisans, shopkeepers, and small moneylenders. And toward the bottom of the pecking order were the laborers in industry, transport, and construction, being mainly Hindi- and Urdu-speaking immigrants from Bihar, the United Provinces, and other parts of northern India, and the servants, cooks, gardeners, sweepers, and other casual workers, for the most part Bengalis and Oriyas.

As a rule, Bengalis were drawn to managerial and skilled jobs. They did not compete with the Bihari, Oriya, and other migrant workers in the jute mills, docks, and railway yards. Even today few of them are rickshaw or handcart pullers, or porters or do other heavy labor. They might enter into activities requiring

greater skills, such as engineering or the manufacture of chemicals and finer textiles. But more typically they made their living
in managerial and clerical positions in commerce, banking, insurance, and real estate. Constituting half the population of Calcutta
in 1964, Bengalis made up more than three-quarters of the city's
middle class and defined the culture and attitudes of the
bhadralok. For them, more than for any other ethnic group, the
city was "home."[19] Because of their disdain for manual labor,
they were also hardest hit in times of economic stagnation, especially the younger, better-educated Bengalis.

The bhadralok looked down upon the wage earners and manual laborers and took little notice of them and their problems.
They had little understanding of the Muslim peasants and the
low-caste Hindu immigrant community, who lived in an entirely
different world from their own. They objected to the wage demands of the palanquin bearers, complaining that money was
being drained out of Bengal by these migrants from Orissa. They
complained that the lack of washermen and their demand for
higher wages were due to the spread of education among the
lower classes. Most of the time, however, bhadralok families
remained distant from the masses and insensitive to the conditions of the poor. Only when it caused inconvenience would they
take notice, such as during the strike by drivers of bullock carts
in 1851 and the milkmen's strike in 1859 "when *sandesh*—the
bhadralok's favorite sweet—disappeared from the market."[20]

The poor, for their part, consisting mainly of unskilled laborers
from various parts of the subcontinent, were fragmented by religion, language, and caste. There were no pressure groups to represent their interests. Except for the occasional riot, Calcutta was
a relatively peaceful city and remained so until the first part of
this century. By the 1920s, associations of white-collar workers
and artisans had become active, and after a series of strikes, trade
unions were set up in the major industries, among jute, port, and
railway workers, for example. The self-employed and indepen-
dent workers, such as rickshaw pullers, cart and carriage drivers,
masons, blacksmiths, and house guards, were more difficult to

organize. In 1930, however, the carters went on strike when the government, prodded by the SPCA, put a ban on the movement of bullock carts during the heat of the day.[21]

Whatever solidarity may have existed among the amorphous mass of the poor was acquired through their popular culture and religion. This culture was expressed in poetry contests, folk art, songs, and comic street shows, often ridiculing "the babus and the dandies, the deceitful Hindu priests and the Christian missionaries." The poor also established their own deities and forms of worship which better addressed their daily concerns, such as the goddess Sitala to ward off cholera and to protect them from smallpox. Their demand for images of these deities even fluctuated with health conditions; when the incidence of smallpox subsided, demand for figures of Sitala went down.

The poor thus remained sharply apart from the bhadralok, who resisted any change to the social order and their privileged status. Black Town itself was split into two distinct societies: bhadralok and *chotalok*—low or vulgar folk—a pejorative term used to evoke a lifestyle to be scrupulously avoided by the educated and privileged Bengalis.

> The typical Calcutta Bengali term *geinya* (meaning rustic simpleton) became current . . . among this new middle class who felt that education in English language and norms alone could set them apart socially from their humble rural origins and associations. The perseverance with which the Christian missionaries, English administrators and educationists drummed into their ears that the Bengalis were a degenerate race, that their social habits and religious practices needed to be discarded and that only the adoption of English language and manners could regenerate them, also motivated these rising Bengali middle classes to dissociate themselves from the lower strata of their community. . . .[22]

Divisions in the social order were mitigated by a patronizing sympathy on the part of the urban elite for their social inferiors. Bhadralok families organized meetings to raise funds for flood relief or to provide medical help during an epidemic. They distributed alms to the poor on religious holidays and on the occasion of a *shradh,* or funeral rite, in one of the houses of the rich. That these acts of benevolence were more than perfunctory expressions of noblesse oblige and reflected any genuine concern for the poor was problematic, to say the least. This is how the local press described (in 1838) the charitable impulses of a wealthy bhadralok family at a time of bereavement:

> For three or four days the poor continued to pour into the town from every venue, like so many files of ants, and were thrust into the houses of nearly seventy of the friends of the family. . . . The distribution of money among the countless beggars who assembled on these occasions can never be conducted with propriety, and invariably entails disgrace. . . . The cause, in the present instance, was the impatience of those in whose house the beggars had been crammed, to get quit of their unwelcome guests; and that many of them opened their gates and liberated the captives before the distributions arrived. . . . That some of the "great beggars" who presided at the distribution of the pittance among the poor beggars . . . suddenly exclaimed that there was not a sufficiency of money; and under pretence of going to the Baboo's house for a further supply, got into their palanquins, and decamped with whatever they could carry off; and that the door-keepers, having waited long for their return in vain, at length liberated the starving and clamorous multitude. Such acts of dishonesty are now invariably practised, whenever a *shradh* is of sufficient magnitude to create confusion and to afford an opportunity for plunder.[23]

At first, the Bengali traders and merchants were concentrated in Burrabazar, the commercial core of north Calcutta. Toward the end of the eighteenth century, however, there was a growing trend among these bhadralok families to withdraw from business. Their joint family system and the long, drawn-out litigation over inheritance inhibited any entrepreneurial drive. Ostentatious living and lavish expenditure on ceremonial occasions left little available for commercial investment. Bengalis soon found that they were losing ground as traders and as bankers to immigrants from different parts of northern India. They turned their attention instead to urban real estate, which provided social prestige as well as greater security for their descendants.

The importance that they gave to houses and land has persisted to the present day. Prestige, for them, depended upon having landlord status, on being a homeowner, not a renter.

> After they had provided houses for themselves [they] went in for house property, which, next to gilt-edged securities, was their favourite investment. They let these houses to those who did not possess houses of their own. These tenants were mostly people whom the true native of Calcutta regarded as resident aliens. But there were also true but poor natives who did not own houses. Their standing in the eyes of their fellow-natives and of their own was mud. They could never console themselves for this deprivation, nor formulate a philosophy of life independent of house property in Calcutta. Thus they were always saving every pice [paisa] they could by scrimping and screwing, until they had saved enough to die as a houseowner. But even those who lived in rented houses disdained to live in flats. They would live only in independent, self-contained houses. . . .[24]

As the prominent Bengali families became *zamindars* or landlords, they were replaced in their mercantile role by Hindi-speaking immigrants, principally Marwaris, who came from the district of Marwar in Rajasthan, a thousand miles away. Marwaris established themselves as the prominent community in Burrabazar by the middle of the nineteenth century, first as bankers and then as traders in cotton goods, jute, grains, opium, spices, and other produce. Lands were purchased in small plots by Marwari traders, who constructed multistoried residential houses with shops on the ground floor and first floor, and the character of Burrabazar and neighboring wards (in Jorashanko and Colutola) changed from a "center of beauty and fashion" to a warren of shops and storage areas devoted exclusively to commerce and trade. Instead of the characteristic large households and languid lifestyle of earlier times, the resident population became overwhelmingly entrepreneurial—

and male—and one part of Burrabazar become notorious as a center of prostitution.

In the past, the Bengal joint family structure linked the urban bhadralok to their rural origins. When attracted to the city by the openings in the British administration, their ties with village relatives were never entirely cut off. The village home was maintained and income pooled from landed rents and urban professional salaries. People from the city returned to the village for religious festivals and family celebrations, and their homes in Calcutta provided lodging for sons of rural relatives and friends for the duration of their schooling.

In the course of the nineteenth century these ties, which "maintained the idle with the earnings of the active," eroded. More or less educated bhadralok youth had to fend for themselves, searching for "decent" employment in subordinate government appointments, teaching posts, and as humble clerks and keepers of wage book and attendance registers in industry, where the term "babu" was applied derogatorily to them by the British. As competition from nonbhadralok immigrants increased, the frustrated ambitions and injured pride of these young bhadralok made them ready recruits for any radical political action. So it would happen, for instance, that Bengali students and unemployed middle-class youth would join with the carters in their 1930 strike against the government.

The so-called Bengali renaissance, which emerged in the late nineteenth century, was a reaction to English rule and modes of Western thought. At that time a major shift took place in the bhadralok system of values. Emphasis was placed on using Bengali, not English, on wearing native clothes, eating native foods, and adopting indigenous medicines. The Swadeshi movement at the beginning of the present century called for a boycott of all British goods and the purchase only of locally produced things. Textile mills, soap factories, tanneries, and cottage industries, such as hand weaving of silk and other fabrics, were set up to meet the needs of the local market. New schools dedicated to nationalism through education were opened, and the circulation of Bengali newspapers soared. "Bengalis were reminded that Kali the Terrible had been created by the gods to destroy demons who would take their kingdom from them, and the parallel was obvious.... Before long there were backyard bomb factories from one end of Calcutta to the other."[25]

This reawakened Bengali nationalism underlay the British decision to partition Bengal in 1905. From then on, the preponderantly Hindu Bengalis of Calcutta found themselves numerically dominated by other ethnic groups whose origin was outside of Bengal. The bhadralok, who had been most vociferously critical of British rule, found themselves isolated. Once the community to whom the city belonged, they became increasingly marginalized as the number of migrants increased, taking up jobs in commerce and industry. More and more offices and industries were owned by people from other states, and migrants were given preference in jobs, leaving fewer opportunities for local people. Calcutta fast became dominated both by outside capital and by an immigrant labor force drawn from all parts of India.

The descendants of the original babus and newcomers to bhadralok status alike had by then acquired a secure income from urban land. They had retreated from life's challenges, from the risks involved in mercantile activities and in the manufacturing opportunities which later developed. They had withdrawn from commerce and had established for themselves instead a sheltered niche in white-collar and professional occupations, which were often linked to colonial rule. Isolated from mainstream productive activity and cut off from the common people, their community stagnated at a time of expansion and growth, its members increasingly pauperized. Less and less able to compete with non-Bengalis, they lost their properties in the core of the city and moved further out, joining the daily flow of commuters to humble white-collar jobs. A sizable part of the Bengali middle class, perhaps 30 percent, became unemployed.[26]

The Bengali parts of Calcutta, both north and south, swept them out in the morning for office work and sucked them back in the evening. They were the men to whom Calcutta belonged by birthright. They loved Calcutta as nobody else did. They lived in it like deep-sea fauna in the depths of the sea. Most of them would have preferred death to being removed from Calcutta.[27]

The process of buying up Bengali property that began in the mid-nineteenth century continues even to the present day. Bengalis complain about Marwaris with money and political connections acquiring houses by fair means and foul and, in the process, destroying the historic character of the city. If they cannot induce Bengalis into selling their ancestral homes by offering large sums of money, they can arrange for *goondas* (the thugs who can always be easily hired in a city of high unemployment) to move in on properties they covet. A typical story is told about how thugs killed the dogs belonging to a Bengali family with a great fondness for pets in an effort to force it to sell out. A series of break-ins, which the police do nothing about, can make life miserable for families sitting on valuable property which they can no longer really afford. Probably retired on a modest civil service pension, cultured and docile by nature, these venerable families are no match against a determined and perhaps ruthless purchaser. To initiate legal action could take years, and elderly owners do not have that many years left. Although sometimes beautiful old mansions are preserved by those Marwaris who like the traditional bungalow architecture, more often developers move in, clear the land, and put up ugly apartment blocks instead. And unable to withstand the inroads of ethnic outsiders and unbridled land speculation, the bhadralok continue their gradual slide into the ranks of Calcutta's dispossessed.

Refugees and Migrants

Over the years, intermittent migration from the villages and towns of Bengal added to the population of Calcutta. At the end of the nineteenth century, agriculture in the surrounding districts came on desperate times. The irrigation system fell into decay and the countryside was ravaged by repeated epidemics of malaria. The city offered hard-pressed peasants and landless laborers a chance for some sort of employment as well as medical treatment and education for their children, which was more than they could get in the villages.

Especially during the nineteenth and early twentieth centuries, enterprising traders from Rajasthan and other parts of India were also establishing themselves in the city. By dint of diligence and ingenuity, they infiltrated into the commercial life of Calcutta, notably within Burrabazar. A newspaper in 1884 described how, arriving with nothing, they would get started and eventually prosper.

> When they first come they bring nothing except a brass drinking pot, tattered clothes, and a big stick. . . . They begin with a capital of two to four annas, buying parched grain and receiving in exchange, not copper or silver coins but pieces of glass or glass bangles, old iron,

35

and other articles, which a needy daughter-in-law or daughter gives away stealthily. This the hawker gathers and sells to bangle-makers and blacksmiths. . . . With the savings of a year or two he opens a small shop, often in partnership with a countryman. . . . If his shop succeeds he gains a share in some cloth-making concern, and at the same time, starts as a moneylender or pawnbroker and rapidly increases his wealth. At this stage in his career he sends for his family and some of his distant relations. . . .[28]

Each ethnic group established its own urban niche, some through trading connections, others through special skills or through manual labor spurned by the native Bengalis. Peasants from Orissa became palanquin bearers or were engaged as domestic servants in Bengali households, because their language and food habits were similar. Rajputs became *darwans*, or gatemen. Biharis took up shoe making and carting.

During the first decades of this century, when Calcutta was a center of Bengali political agitation, the British encouraged Marwari traders to move into economically strategic positions previously held by Bengalis. Rajasthani commercial castes entered into industry as well as into foreign trade; Gujaratis, with their ties in Bombay, into the textile, timber, and tobacco trades; Sikhs into transport; and other Punjabis into commerce and industry.[29] As one of India's more dynamic industrial centers, Calcutta drew scores of thousands of laborers, turning it into a city of migrants—a large dormitory of sorts, where residence was temporary and civic commitment was nil. Before long, migrants constituted nearly half of the population of the city.

Occupational grouping by place of origin still holds true today. Migrants from the same states tend to be found in the same occupations. Those from Bihar and Uttar Pradesh are disproportionately concentrated in factory employment or in work as rickshaw pullers. Orissa accounts for a majority of the city's plumbers, carpenters, gardeners, and *pan*—betel nut —stall keepers. Taxi drivers are still frequently Punjabis. The jute industry is manned to a large extent by Bihari and Uttar Pradesh Muslims. The engineering industry contains a high concentration of

Bengali Hindus. City dwellers also live in communal pockets, each ethnic group tending to cluster in a particular location. Generally, Hindi speakers are Hindus, and Urdu speakers are Muslims, so religion as well as language and place of origin determine the work that one does in the city.

The push of rural misery, it seems, has been more of a factor in migration than the pull of urban opportunity. During the First World War, when exploitation of the hinterland of Calcutta intensified, the number of impoverished migrants coming into the city sharply increased. What was referred to as "the beggar nuisance" attracted the attention of the citizens of Calcutta, especially the European residents. Beggars were arrested and sent to prison, only to resume begging immediately after their release. It was deemed to be an offense, punishable with imprisonment, to beg for alms in any public place, "or to expose or exhibit any sores, wounds, bodily ailment or deformity, with the object of exciting charity, or of attaining alms." With a term in jail being welcome to most beggars, it came as no surprise that the law had little effect in curbing the nuisance.

The Bengal famine of 1943 unleashed new waves of rural destitutes upon the city. The famine, the like of which had not been experienced since 1770, was largely due to poor rice harvests and the cutoff of supplies from Burma, then in Japanese hands. Hoarding and profiteering on an unprecedented scale drove prices up. Three and a half million persons died. Thousands of men, women, and children poured into the city from the countryside. The residential quarters of the city began to ring late in the evening with the heart-rending cries of famished beggars pleading for the rice drainings from the kitchens of the more fortunate. Caste rules were disregarded. Hindus received cooked food and gruel from the Muslim homes with little thought given to ritual restrictions. Family life was shattered. Husbands abandoned wives. Wives left ailing husbands at home. Parents left immature children to their fate or left babies at the gates of wealthy households and drifted away to seek food. Widowed sisters, who had been living with the families of their brothers, were asked to leave, even when they had no place else to go. The mayor of Calcutta appealed for help:

> In panic and despair hungry mothers from the mofussil [rural districts] with suckling babies in their bosom, famished fathers with starving children in their arms, have streamed into the city of Calcutta in search of a few morsels of food. Men, women and children, struggling for their very existence have very often been found picking up refuse from the dustbins in the city, just to keep up their miserable life which is fast flickering out. Many a time man and dog have fought over the same bit of food across the streets. Our mothers and sisters appear today in tattered clothes ... hardly sufficient to cover their shame.[30]

The government "repatriated" some forty thousand persons to the countryside, often to localities distant from their original homes. Others left the city on their own accord as famine conditions subsided. The distressing street scenes gradually disappeared, and the horrors of famine had little lasting impact. But their shadow has persisted in memory.

Not so with the flood of refugees from erstwhile East Bengal. This influx, which began with Partition and has continued intermittently ever since, has had a profound impact on the city. The first arrivals appeared in 1948, and in the years that immediately followed, the numbers surged because of continuing disturbances and horrendous stories of atrocities perpetrated on the Hindu minority in what had become East Pakistan. The initial waves were made up mainly of bhadralok who had worked in public service or in trade, rather than peasants who worked on the land. Cultivators could scarcely risk migrating to places where lands would not be available to them. Three-quarters of the migrants were caste Hindus, the rest largely untouchables. Nearly half of them settled in urban areas where there were opportunities to engage in petty trade and cottage industry.[31]

The city was totally unprepared to receive this inundation. In the absence of any longer-term policy for dealing with them, refugees who sought government help were kept in relief camps, where conditions were appalling. In the southern and northern suburbs, many of them began occupying empty buildings and lands, and squatter colonies sprang up in many places.

Before this influx of refugees, new arrivals to Calcutta would find accommodation in the bustees, shifting from one bustee to another when they were evicted. But with refugees crowding in, there was no more room in the bustees, leaving little choice but to put up some makeshift shelter wherever space could be found. Government efforts to settle them were halting and halfhearted. The initial concentrations were in the Dum Dum suburb (where the airport is located) and in south Calcutta. As these areas became filled, refugees moved onto small vacant plots nearer the center of the city or onto marshy low-lying areas on the periphery. When the government tried to acquire lands for them at modest prices, landowners would file injunctions in the law courts to frustrate the effort, and land prices soared because of the ever-increasing demand. Unable to provide alternative accommodation, as it had promised, the government looked on as eviction notices were issued, although these were only sporadically enforced. Nearly five hundred refugee families remained permanently encamped upon the platforms of the Sealdah railroad station until 1956, when they were shifted into some vacant film studios and into the godown of a disused jute mill, where they remained for another decade.[32]

Despite a common Bengali tradition and Hindu religion, the refugees from East Bengal were not easily assimilated into the wider community. This was partly due to their firm adherence to their former status, constantly harking back to the past and to pleasant memories of home life and native soil. Many of the refugees had been forced to sell their homes at rock-bottom prices or abandon them altogether, leaving furniture, iron gates, doorknobs, and other fixtures behind for the taking. Having given up everything that meant most to them, including family shrines and traditions, they now had to live in dreary quarters and depend on relatives or charity, with little hope of finding work.

They were not welcomed by the native Bengali community,

whose city it was supposed to be. The once-proud bhadralok middle class, "ground down by unemployment and poverty, was the angriest of all" and did not take kindly to the refugee intrusion. They looked down upon them as people who had defiled their city and referred to them disparagingly as "Bengals." Middle-class indifference to the plight of refugees was felt from the moment of their first arrival in Calcutta.

> The thousands of commuters, who daily poured into the platforms of Sealdah station, barely noticed the faces blackened with grime and sweat. They carefully avoided contact with the dirtied bodies of this unwanted crowd. . . . The refugees stood like Ruth amid the alien corn . . . prey to crooks of every description. . . .[33]

Before the refugees arrived, the renting out of any extra rooms provided the bhadralok with a means of getting some income. When new tenants moved in, rents could be legally increased. Then the presence of thousands of refugees created a tremendous surge in demand for housing. Tenants stayed put and rents became frozen. Relations between owners and tenants deteriorated, and maintenance of properties was neglected. There was no longer any incentive to build rental housing. The situation became increasingly desperate, especially for widows and hard-pressed families who depended on rents for income, and the refugees were blamed.

After the Indo-Pakistan war in 1964, more refugees poured in to escape political uncertainty and religious strife in East Pakistan. From 1946 to the mid-seventies, 4.2 million East Pakistanis registered as refugees in West Bengal, the annual influx reaching peaks of 925,000 in 1950 and 667,000 in 1964. Then, once again, in the wake of the 1971 war between East and West Pakistan, another 7.5 million refugees entered West Bengal. By 1972, however, about 6 million of them had returned to the newly created nation of Bangladesh.

The refugees experienced the trauma of sudden impoverishment. Their world had come to an end. They had to fend for themselves, some in government camps, many more as squatters on other people's land, living in empty buildings or in improvised shelters of bamboo matting or tin walls and a roof made of tin sheets or sacks and straw mats weighed down by stones. Theirs was a double displacement, not only from their ancestral locale but also from respectable bhadralok status and middle-class aspirations. They bemoaned the forcible transition from open fields and wide-flowing rivers to an urban life of penury and degradation. Most of them were literate, besides having some technical or handicraft skill. Those who had hoped to engage in trading had to put up with clerical or unskilled manual work. Those with professional qualifications had to become street hawkers or small shop owners. For unemployed refugee youth with a secondary or higher education, adapting to the new circumstances was especially traumatic and demeaning.[34]

Most of the 2.4 million refugees who had settled in and around Calcutta since Partition were eventually absorbed in middle-class neighborhoods or in the bustees. But some half million of them remained in dispersed refugee colonies where—eventually—their occupation and rights to rehabilitation were recognized. Many of them received title to their plots, but only 2.5 *cottahs* of land (about 1800 square feet) and a pitifully inadequate house-building grant must have been disheartening after the more comfortable circumstances they had known in the past. This security of tenure, however, made a fundamental difference: it provided the incentive that was needed to set in motion a process of improving their living conditions. The houses were, for the most part, individually owned, single-dwelling units. Some of the colonies were eventually provided with roads, drains, lights, water taps, and other infrastructure, and many of them became indistinguishable from other middle-class neighborhoods. Because of the security of tenure they confer, refugee colonies are now looked upon as an urban success story.

The investment by refugees in housing also reflected their growing commitment to the city. They had arrived with families mainly intact. In spite of the utter disorder and uprooting from their social and economic moorings, they maintained a high de-

gree of kinship solidarity. Cherished memories of a better life in
the past did not prevent their eventual identification with the city
with which they shared religion, language, and culture. They
were also prepared to enter into types of manual work traditionally spurned by Bengalis, as bicycle rickshaw operators and as
drivers of taxis, buses, and trucks.

Eventually, the 562 refugee colonies located in the Calcutta
Metropolitan District included a total of some 90,000 family
plots or a population of about half a million. Some of the colonies were located on government land. Others were "regularized"
by the government after compensating the landowners on behalf
of the squatters. Many of the plot holders were provided with
leases for ninety-nine years in consideration of payment of an
annual ground rent. Banks, however, did not always come forward with mortgage loans on the strength of such leases, even
when the land was centrally located and valuable.[35]

Refugee success in agitating against eviction was due largely
to pressure from a coalition of refugees and leftist political parties. Calcutta was described at the time as being "a city of processions, a nightmare city of one big rally after another." The
Left Front Government, which has been in power since 1977,
still draws major support at election times from the refugee community. Whenever tenants or squatters confront landlords or
other authorities regarding their rights, the government usually
backs the refugees, and when the case is decided, compensates
the landlords.

Migrants come to the city under conditions quite different from
refugees. Those from the rural districts of West Bengal, having
lost their land to moneylenders, floods, or other disasters, sometimes arrive as whole families and maintain only weak linkages
with their place of origin. The majority of migrants, however,
coming mainly from Bihar and elsewhere in northern India, leave
wives and children behind in their home villages, where they
retain close ties and regularly return. So there are two distinct
categories: permanent and temporary migrants. They possess al-

together different perspectives, which ultimately shape their slum life and relationship with the dominant society.

Migrants come to the city for the express purpose of getting work, however low-paying. The move is often made out of desperation: "When landlord oppression had snatched the last bit of land and last beast of burden from the peasant Gaffar, only then did he think of the jute mills. It was an act of absolute despair, almost of suicide."[36]

If only because of the cost of living and lack of accommodation, many migrants cannot bring their wives and children with them. Instead, they return to their villages every year to see families and kinsmen, timing their visit to coincide with peak agricultural activities when there is work to be done. Although some of them may end up residing in Calcutta for many years, the city is seen as simply a place of work and nothing more, a place in which they have no permanent stake. They send out, year after year, their savings through small postal remittances to relatives at home. Like it or not, it has been on the toil of these men who have left families at home that the economy of the city has been based, making Calcutta perhaps the most male city in the world. There are three males to every two women.

Early in this century when jute and other industries were being established, there were two females for every five male immigrants living in the city. According to the 1911 census, a quarter of the women who were listed as employed were prostitutes.

Had the possibility of a decent family life existed, more migrants would have brought their families with them. There was no compelling reason, however, to make this possible. It was in the interest of the mill managers to have a largely floating labor force always available and willing to work for a pittance. Technical and managerial jobs were reserved for Europeans, and clerical work was done by Bengali babus. The average jute mill manager, "usually a kindly Scot from Dundee," had little awareness of the condition of his employees. Skill requirements were minimal and literacy irrelevant. Any required proficiency could be acquired very quickly, so workers remained highly replaceable. Poorly housed and never fully "urbanized," this casual labor force would be replenished as needed from the bottomless manpower pool that was to be found in the overpopulated states of north India.[37]

> Urban slums, seasonal migration and the poor and temporary quality of labour, were all a function of keeping down the wages of labour to an extraordinarily low level of subsistence. The labour force, drawn from different provinces, castes and communities, continued to live in the city . . . as isolated social groups with no widespread communication among themselves. The working-class quarters seethed with tensions between different communities, which on a few occasions flared into communal riots. The predominantly rural and migratory character of labour, and the survival of traditional identities among them, hindered the growth of proletarian political consciousness and class solidarity.[38]

Migrants accept accommodation in a bleak tenement or a single room, ill lit and without ventilation or cooking arrangements, or in shop dwellings in either their own shop or their employer's place of business, or on the street, a veranda, or beneath the stairs, with the roadside water tap as the main source of water, the sidewalk as the kitchen, and the drains as their lavatory. The pan wallah conducts his daily business on a raised platform, below which he may have his combined bed and kitchen. The rickshaw wallah sleeps in the garage where his rickshaw is stored or lives with ten others like himself cooped in a single, shared room. Under these cramped conditions, family life becomes impossible. Without the comforts and restraints of a normal family life, prostitution and vice run rampant. When violence occurs, it is attributed in part to the fact that there are so many men without women in the city.

Because migrants come to the city expressly to get work, there is little unemployment to be found among them. They are never idle. Unskilled and arriving in Calcutta alone, or with their families, they take whatever work they can find, be it as coolies, office peons, washermen, cobblers, hawkers, construction laborers, rickshaw pullers, garage assistants, bus conductors, cooks, maid servants, midwives, tea stall boys, sweepers, prostitutes, or ragpickers. Unemployment is a luxury they cannot afford. Unable to find any job after a few months, they go elsewhere in search of work or else they return to their home villages.

The transfer of rural poverty to the city is most glaring among those who live on Calcutta's crumbling sidewalks. Featured in every film or report, the thousands who make their home on the street have become a cliché for hopelessness. To alien eyes they epitomize all that is wrong with the city. The visitor sees these destitutes lying upon the ground like little bundles of rags and reacts with shock and revulsion at the spectacle of such utter impoverishment. There may be 200,000 of them, even more by some estimates, depending on the season.

Migrants take up life on the pavements for a variety of reasons: flood, a dispute with a landlord, the death of parents, family tensions, eviction, or they may just prefer to sleep "in the comparatively open air of the streets rather than stifle in the foetid atmosphere of a Calcutta slum." Among them are sojourners who come to the city during the agricultural slack period before the monsoon, leaving families in the countryside. The majority of them, however, come as whole families from Calcutta's immediate hinterland where there are perennial crop failures and close links to the city because of suburban railway lines and roads. Migrant women work as domestic servants or as ragpickers collecting recyclable wastes from the garbage dumps. Also among these pavement dwellers are regular visitors to the city who sell rice, green coconuts, and vegetables or work as snake charmers, astrologers, and palmists. There are groups of adolescent boys who do not know where to live, who collect paper and rags, waste vegetables from the markets, firewood and small bits of charcoal along the railway tracks to sell as fuel, or metal scraps and other refuse from garbage bins. Some of them end up as pimps for the keepers of prostitutes or as agents for criminals. There are young girls driven by life in the streets into the net of the seasoned madams who run houses of prostitution.

Inevitably there are the beggars, the sick, the infirm, the physically handicapped. The individual situations of sidewalk dwellers defy generalization. When, because of age or infirmity, earning capabilities drop too low, stark destitution forces the person or family into the most marginal vocation of all, that of begging.

> He came to Calcutta about seven years ago. He worked as a porter at Sealdah station, and with the little earning managed to maintain his family. But it was extremely troublesome for him to live on the station platform with his wife and young children. Hence, he shifted from the station, and finally settled in Hazra Park area. Now he is a professional beggar. His wife gave birth to a daughter only two months ago, right on the pavement of Hazra Road.[39]

They fight over a patch of space or over waste food distributed by a hotel at night, but when it rains, one sidewalk dweller gets help from another. They try to lead ordinary lives, cooking their own food and changing their location only when forced to do so. They wash on the street, where they are also shaved and barbered. They are offered food and clothing by families and restaurants in the neighborhood. They will not miss handouts from charities, neighborhood welfare committees, or from the trustees of rich feudal families. Their needs, however, are by no means restricted to the bare essentials for survival. They respect religious customs and rituals, and marriages are arranged between socially equivalent families living on the pavements. The vitality of their social and cultural institutions even under such austere economic circumstances has been cited as a major feature of life among the urban poor.[40]

The common belief that migrants coming to the city first occupy pavements before moving into slums is for the most part erroneous. Many migrants consider the sidewalks as their urban residence, as a way of life and a reasonably organized one at that. They have their preferred locations near markets where work can be had, or at major intersections, or under arcades providing shelter from the rain, or in parks and playgrounds for their daily necessities. For the self-employed, earning opportunities are invariably location-specific—tea shop keepers, vegetable vendors, hawkers, sweepers, shoeshine boys, cobblers, even temple priests—work where they can capture a strategic location. Men and women working in construction will live with their work-mates in the building under construction or under an arcade near the work site. Handcart and rickshaw pullers need to have a parking space for their vehicles, which they must keep an eye on to protect against theft. Spending the night near a source of employment ensures that the porter or handcart puller will be available at the first beck and call of possible employers. Congested parts of the city, such as wholesale markets, dockyards, and railway stations offer the best opportunities to earn a livelihood by selling labor services in highly competitive environments.

Sidewalk dwellers consequently tend to cluster in the central business district, occupying some of the most expensive real estate in the city. It is simplistic to talk of providing shelter for the homeless, Calcutta officials conclude. Night shelters have been proposed where sidewalk dwellers can sleep for a nominal payment, but getting suitable buildings that are centrally located is next to impossible. Nor has any progress been made on a plan to establish night clinics. Other than installing a few "pay-and-use toilets," little has been accomplished in the way of ameliorating the conditions of persons living on the streets.

After all the studies and discussions are over, the problem of homelessness in Calcutta remains as intractable as ever. It is possible to deal with refugees and slum dwellers in a squatter settlement or a bustee. At least their locations are fixed. But those who are reduced to scrounging space on the streets live anonymously in the shadows, never clearly identified and defined. Dispersed physically as well as sociologically, they do not form an effective constituency from which a group consciousness can emerge and bring pressure to bear on city officials. They cannot even be counted for that matter, much less interviewed, except late at night. At other times there is nothing to distinguish them from the hawkers and others who make their livings on the streets.

Slums and Squatters

In Calcutta, the distinguishing feature of a slum are *kutcha* structures, meaning those built mainly of mud brick, bamboo, or thatch. The term, which derives from the word for "crude" or "unripe," refers to a house that is makeshift, flimsy, and unfinished, as opposed to *pucca,* the widely known Indian expression which derives from "mature" or "cooked" and which means built with good materials and designed to endure. If the slum is legally recognized and registered, it is known as a bustee, and bustee holdings, which are the units for purposes of registration, are taxed. Otherwise, it is a squatter colony, officially illegal and universally disparaged.

Slums in Indian cities do not develop near the city center, as they do in the United States, where property taken over by the poor has been abandoned by more affluent citizens, who have moved to the suburbs. In India, slums spring up throughout the city, wherever there are markets, shops, factories, middle-class homes, and even in posh residential areas—any place in need of cheap labor and services. Although the immediate environment deteriorates because of the crowding and pollution, wealthy and middle-class families, including those who have fallen on hard times, hang on to their properties.

The symbiotic relationship between rich and poor was originally expressed in the warren of bazaars and hutments which grew up around the mansions of the babu elite. The relationship between multistory masonry buildings, known as *kothabari,* and kutcha bustees is a modern variant of this development. In some places there is a mix of bustees and four-story blocks, originally built as government housing but which have become badly overcrowded as renters have sublet space to poor families.

Climbing up the dark staircase of one of these buildings, past sleeping dogs sprawled on the landings, refuse pushed against grimy, betel-stained walls, and doors left ajar to capture whatever ventilation there is, one catches glimpses into small, gloomy apartments where conditions are certainly no better than in a claustrophobic hut in a bustee. Water is lugged upstairs in a bucket, cooking done over a charcoal and dung fire set up on a landing, clothing placed to dry on a roof that is accessible only by means of a tottery stepladder made of bamboo.

In the early days of Calcutta, the gentry made land available for putting up huts to be rented out to migrant artisans and laborers, whose contribution to the economy was of paramount importance. Otherwise, the poor invaded open lands near wherever there was demand for their labor, even if the land was not fit for human habitation. They appropriated swampy, low-lying areas, borders of drainage channels, and vacant plots under bridges or on berms alongside railway tracks. Because of this inexorable encroachment of slums on space normally reserved for other purposes, Calcutta has often been depicted as being but "one big slum."

Crumbling elegance stands cheek by jowl with improvised huts of the meanest sort, all of which is overlaid by a patina of grime and decay. There is no concealing the conditions of the poor, no blotting out their wretchedness. They are not isolated in ghettos or hidden away behind high walls or on the other side of railroad tracks. The Bengali novelist Amitav Ghosh described what he saw as a boy when he looked out from an upstairs window of a relative's apartment:

The ground fell away sharply from the edges of the building and then leveled out into a patchwork of stagnant pools, dotted with islands of low, raised ground. Clinging to these islands were little clumps of shanties, their beaten tin roofs glistening rustily in the midday sun. The pools were black, covered with a sludge so thick that it had defeated even the ubiquitous carpets of water hyacinth. I could see women squatting at the edges of the pools, splashing with both hands to drive back the layers of sludge, scooping up the cleaner water underneath to scrub their babies and wash their clothes and cooking utensils. . . .[41]

The scene he described was from Jadevpur in south Calcutta at a time when there was still vacant land on which refugees could build. In Calcutta's north side—the Black Town of the bad old days—the scene would have been quite different. The streets there are narrow and congested, and upper-floor apartments look down on the tile roofs of small pockets of one-story bustees. Often hidden away are the grand houses which once belonged to Bengali babus and Marwari merchants, with their Corinthian pillars, arches, ornate balconies, and balustrades chipped and begrimed, yet still largely intact. Where the structure abuts a principal street, the ground floors have been taken over by stores, workshops, tea stalls, and small warehouses. Maintenance has been neglected over the years, and decay may be so complete that vines and stunted, misshapen trees grow out of the rotting, lichen-encrusted masonry, as if entire structures are imperceptibly reverting back to the clays from which they were originally built.

Many of these ancestral houses are subdivided into tiny apartments and have taken on a tenement-like appearance. In this way, low-rent housing is created by breaking up existing dwellings to accommodate additional families. Typically, two-room apartments face a veranda that wraps around a central shaft, being all that remains of the inner courtyard of the original edifice, or else the verandas and open spaces have been converted into living rooms and kitchens. Toilets are shared by a number of families, and water is obtained in a bucket from a street-level tap. Cooking is done on the floor of a narrow, connecting hall or on the veranda, the smoldering fuel balls of mud and coal dust in the chula sending up acrid clouds of smoke, which choke the floors above. Rented out to lower-middle-class bhadralok families, these apartments often serve the dual purpose of living quarters and workshops.

Where large residences are located close to the river and thus accessible to cheap transport, the ground floors have been given over to warehouses; machine shops, or small factories for spinning and weaving cotton, and on the upper floors, wherever you look, a beehive of activity: lathes and grinders at work turning out spindles or bushings (light engineering being an area in which Bengalis predominate), printing and print making, the assembly of cartons and boxes, working in plastic, and myriad other cottage industries.

In a city where space is at a premium, it seems incongruous to come upon a once-elegant structure shuttered and empty, the gate padlocked, the garden unkempt and gone to seed. Retained by the family, the house is too valuable to subject to the wear and tear that goes with renting, yet too costly to maintain as a single-family residence. In some cases the house remains occupied with its integrity more or less preserved by partitioning the ground floor into apartments and turning the rear garden into a backyard to be used for drying clothes and raising some chickens. The apartments are rented out to families, leaving the elderly descendants of the original owner to putter about through the musty rooms of the floor above. These houses, with their lofty ceilings and overhead fans blackened with grime, threadbare furniture, old books and memorabilia, a small black-and-white TV in one corner, a large framed picture of Rabindranath Tagore along with solemn portraits of distinguished ancestors and Hindu holy men on the walls, echo memories of old Calcutta and its bhadralok heritage.

Available housing stock could never keep pace with the growth of population unless converted into slums through extensive subletting. During the nineteenth century, the number of houses increased by one-fifth, while the population increased fivefold. As the number of pucca houses grew, the number of kutcha huts of the poor actually diminished. Densities rose dramatically. The city saw the breakup of large houses in which extended families had once lived and a rapid increase in the number of rented premises. Several households were accommodated in a structure which earlier had been the residence of the owner and his married sons and other relatives. The average number of persons per house rose from 2.6 in 1821 to 7.6 in 1901.[42]

Displaced from their homes within the city, the poor were forced to seek shelter on the outskirts or to crowd in elsewhere. Municipal regulations required that all straw huts be cleared away so as to prevent fires. The huts of the poor were demolished when streets were widened or when space was needed for tramway company stables or a jute warehouse. The improvement of the riverfront called for the removal of private residences and their conversion into godowns, which also disrupted the livelihoods of families who had clustered around these residences to provide services. Under the pressures of development, this displacement of the poor continued. The buying up of bustee land in the 1880s benefited landowners and developers, but certainly not the bustee dwellers. They had to move elsewhere. By then, much of the city's daily population—the domestic servants, water carriers, artisans, transporters, jute and textile workers, and others on whom the city depended—had already been pushed out to the edges.

Since the turn of the century, there has been little change in these trends. Densities in the bustees increased inexorably as kutcha structures were replaced by pucca units and new stories added. For the evicted tenants who could not afford the higher rents, there was no place to turn. Even the building of multistory apartments, which began in the 1960s, did not free up much space for the poor. When families who could afford the new apartments moved, the vacated premises were taken over by friends and or by the landlord, thus adding little to the housing stock available to lower-income families.[43]

When there was no land in the city proper on which new slums could develop, improvised shelters—known locally as *jhopris*—set up in fringe areas on public land provided the only alternative. Choice of location depended on access to livelihoods. In the 1970s, the area on the eastern fringe now known as Salt Lake City was developed by landfill, and new houses and government offices were built there. There was no public transport or markets at first, creating an ideal opportunity for squatters: the ready availability of jobs for men as day laborers, rickshaw pullers, bicycle van drivers, and vegetable sellers and for women as maidservants and cooks. In no time at all, their shacks began sprouting amidst the new buildings in what had been planned originally as a slum-free suburb.

Squatter colonies have been an intrinsic part of the Calcutta landscape since the time of Partition. Lands belonging to the government, the railway, and private individuals were overwhelmed by refugees, creating scenes that were filled with foreboding:

> Dusty streets straggle away in every direction, lined with tiny shacks built of metal scraps, pieces of old baskets, strips of wood, and gunny sacks. In the dark interiors of the shacks, small fires glow though the smoke, and dark faces gaze out at children playing in the urinous-smelling, fly-infested streets. In a few years the children who survive . . . will grow taller and thinner and stand in the streets like ragged skeletons, barefoot, hollow-eyed, blinking their apathetic stares out of gray, dusty faces.[44]

The government regularized some of the refugee colonies, but nothing was seriously done to arrest their proliferation. To evict refugees was politically unacceptable and, as a practical matter, depended upon the availability of suitable alternative locations, of which there were none. Over the years, the colonies have continued to multiply. In addition to refugees, they have become filled by Bengalis from the rural districts near Calcutta, mainly agricultural laborers and peasants who lost their land in times of drought or flood, or by "up-country" non-Bengalis from other states in India or by Bangladeshi Muslims, who have raised their shacks just as Hindu refugees did in the past. For the more recent arrivals, there was great difficulty in finding space. Without relatives already established, access became virtually impossible.

According to the Slum Areas (Improvement and Clearance) Act of 1972, these shantytowns are illegal because of conditions that are "injurious to public health or safety or morals of the inhabitants." The law notwithstanding, 150,000 people are said to be living in these unauthorized settlements within the greater metropolitan area. And these are only in the larger and obvious congeries. Probably this many more are tucked away in crevices between buildings and in the lean-tos which hug walls adjacent to public water taps, bus terminals, and major intersections.

Many of the older settlements enjoy the protection of political leaders. In return for reasonable security of occupancy and access to water taps, which politicians can easily arrange, the squatters are expected to attend local political rallies, chant slogans, and join in protests and processions. Proper political behavior earns them the ration cards that allow them to obtain government surplus grain and cooking oil and establish legal residency and the right to vote.

Their settlements are more organized than they seem to the outsider. The jumble of shelters appears to be haphazard and random, but in fact the allocation of land has been carefully managed from the start. This is how the first colonies were established after Partition:

> The land, identified in advance, would usually be occupied under cover of night; plots would be marked off, and shacks erected with incredible speed, thatched with the *hogla* leaves which became an emblem of squatter life. Young girls were often left in charge of the newly-set-up hearth to forestall violent eviction. Subscriptions and joint labour, supervised by the colony committee, went into clearing the land and laying down roads, drains and a water supply.[45]

Squatter colonies today have important political links. They constitute a "vote bank" for the party of their patrons. A mafia godfather and *dadas* ("elder brothers" in the vernacular) who have connections act as intermediaries between the squatters, politicians, and police. They mediate disputes and fix matters with the authorities. Although not part of the establishment, they organize the colony for political purposes and wield considerable influence. On private land, a pirate developer will provide security and space in return for payments, which are used to bribe officials whose duty it is to clear illegal settlements.

Due to their illegal status, squatters occupy a blind spot in official statistics. Little hard information is available about them. What is known comes from private surveys that have been conducted in a few particular settlements. These show that most squatters are self-employed in making such items as boxes, paper packets, wooden spoons for ice cream, cow dung cakes, and fuel balls from a mixture of coal dust, hay, and clay, or as hawkers, rickshaw and cart pullers, and scavengers. Somewhat fewer of them have "regular" paying unskilled jobs as ticket takers on buses, in construction, and whatnot. Many of the women are engaged in domestic service, the lowest-paying work of all. Even beggars are said to earn more than they do. Two-thirds of earnings goes for food, and some families pay rent or some recompense to local leaders or the employees of municipal authorities to avoid being forcibly evicted. The readiness to pay anything at all on a regular basis merely to retain the right to subsist under such deplorable conditions is tragic testament to their plight.

The authorities look upon their miserable shacks as eyesores, as obstructing pedestrians, as hazards to health, as illegal use of public land without paying taxes. They are referred to in Bengali as *jabar dakhal,* literally "forcibly occupied." In the popular perception they represent willful defiance of the law and civilized norms by "antisocial" elements. Squatters become the inevitable scapegoats when there is a crime or disturbance. Especially if Bangladeshis, they are denigrated as petty smugglers, prostitutes, pickpockets, and drug traffickers. Because of this image, they cannot expect much protection from the police. Indeed, they are at the mercy of the police, who sanction their illegal existence.

However, incidents of police brutality, including rape, will sometimes provoke an upsurge of public indignation. Looking out for their vote bank, local bosses and dadas may pressure the government to take action. Most likely the subinspector of police will be transferred to another precinct, and the matter will be forgotten until the next incident occurs.

Acquiring land to widen a road, put up a building, dredge a canal, or plant trees entails the removal of squatters. Heated controversy invariably ensues, sometimes accompanied by violence. Squatters constitute an established community, however precarious their condition may seem. They may have ration cards and even have mail delivered to their pitiful homes. They provide services which the surrounding neighborhood cannot do without. By law, they should be given written notice and sufficient time to show why they should not be evicted, but the law is not always applied. By law, they should also be given a place to resettle, but they cannot survive on promises alone.

When it comes to a showdown, the squatters often prevail. Once, in the port area of Kidderpore, they made their stand. Women and children stood in the vanguard in order to forestall any concerted charge by the police with their *lathis,* the bamboo staves that they use to beat crowds into submission. This show of defiance was enough to prevent bringing up a bulldozer to clear away the shacks. The dismantling was begun instead by hand (which at least allowed the recovery of asbestos roofing, which could fetch a good price in the market). In the meantime, the squatters obtained through their local political connections a restraining order, and their community, at least for the time being, was left alone.

Where there is political and neighborhood support, squatters may enjoy reasonable security of tenure. There is even a law on the books which stipulates that squatters cannot be evicted after twelve years of continuous occupancy. That a colony is favored is evident from the physical conditions: tiled roofs instead of sacks and straw mats, a well installed by the municipality, some trees that have been planted, a school started with some private funds. A location next to babu apartment buildings ensures some neighborhood concern for conditions in a Bengali colony. If a senior government official lives close by, so much the better. But if the upper apartments belong to Bengalis who overlook a slum occupied by Urdu-speaking "up-country" people, the different cultures militate against such supportive relationships.

Unnayan (Progress) and Chhinnamul Sramajibi Adhikar Samiti (Uprooted Day Laborers Rights Committee) are two private voluntary organizations that act as advocates for squatter rights. They conduct inquiries into why policies are not being enforced, and they organize demonstrations. The cases they raise, however, can remain hung up in the courts for years. In the mid-1980s, some one hundred families who had been peacefully living for thirty years on municipal land in Baghbazar in north Calcutta were notified of their pending eviction. The land was needed in order to construct a multistory apartment block. Unnayan negotiated with the municipality, which promised that another site would be made available where the families could relocate, but this was not done. Eviction led to violence involving injuries, and some squatters were taken into police custody. The site was cleared and construction began, but it was stopped when the judge issued an injunction, and for years the situation remained in stalemate.

Gobindapur Rail Colony Gate 1 is strung out along the railway tracks near Dhakuria in south Calcutta. It began some fifty years ago when a shopkeeper, who had the business of recycling used glass bottles and vials, built some shacks on railway land and, as the new zamindar, persuaded migrant families from rural West Bengal to rent them from him. Later, some people with ties to the political left extended this invasion of railway lands, renting out additional plots, this time to East Bengal migrants. The railway authorities tried to do away with the settlement because it encroached upon the right-of-way. They planned initially to build a wall around the colony but later relented and decided instead to put up barbed wire fencing between the squatters and the tracks so as to restrict movement across the right-of-way. But the tracks, against which the squatter huts abutted, served as an important thoroughfare, binding the colony together and providing access to the narrow interior passages. The tracks also provided a place to meet, sit, play, dry clothes, and perform other chores. With support from local communist activists, the community was able to thwart repeatedly the plans of the railway authorities. The key to its success was organization and political connections.

A "people's welfare committee" had been formed under a dynamic leader who had an aptitude for producing folk operas and for teaching the local children, even though his own education was little above the primary level. His good relations with some politicians and policemen in the area secured their support when there were confrontations with the railway. The committee also served other functions. People would come to it with their disputes and family quarrels or for help and advice in case of illness. It maintained the local shrine of the goddess Sitala and organized the Sitala puja, the biggest festival in the colony, to which all the residents contributed. It also lobbied the municipality to put in some water taps and latrines.

Most of the residents still live below the poverty line. The men work as shop hands, helpers on minibuses, and casual laborers in construction, house painting, or *pandal* making and decoration during festivals. Suffering from chronic insecurity and changing jobs frequently, they are unable to progress to higher-paying work. The women find employment as domestic servants in nearby middle-class residential areas. With more regular earnings, they end up assuming the main responsibility for supporting the family. Young girls go out with their mothers in the morning to help with the chores. Young boys get jobs as helpers in tea shops, garages, or in car cleaning.

Each family lives in a single room, its furniture consisting of little more than a wooden cot with the bedding kept on it and a suitcase or trunk. One or two ropes on which clothing is hung are slung across the room on one side. Utensils are left on the floor where cooking is done. A calendar with the picture of gods or goddesses hangs on the wall.

> Most adult males and females go out to work in the morning. They have rice cooked overnight and steeped in water. The children also eat the same food in the morning. . . . The women return by midday. The children share any food which their mothers may bring from the work place. . . . The male members, who stay out of their homes for work, have some food within their means at midday. . . . Only one full meal for all is provided at night after the return of males from work. . . .
>
> By 4 P.M. the entire area along the railway tracks is full of women and children of the colony. An observer is struck by the mood of relaxation in all of them. It is as if the rail tracks doubly represent a domestic compound and a public ensemble. The women talk among themselves sitting on the railway tracks. Some of them can be seen combing their hair while talking merrily with one another. A number of vendors throng the area during these hours. This is how the tracks turn into a promenade for the children, some of whom are enabled by the mothers to have tidbits like very cheap ice-cream, *kulfi*, fried chickpea, monkey nuts and things like that.[46]

In the Tiljala area of east Calcutta there is an improved bustee with water taps and other utilities. Immediately behind, a line of improvised shacks hugs the railway embankment where Muslims from Bihar have been living for a decade or more. A muddy path, along which people pass in single file, separates two lines of dark, windowless hovels made of bamboo and thatch, with dirt floors, tin or tile roofs. Illegally connected electric lines are strung out along the path. Inside the huts, the only furniture is a bed, raised on bricks so that the children can sleep underneath. Because there are no water taps, residents cross over into the nearby bustee at times when the bustee dwellers have finished drawing water for their own needs. This is done by the women, who bring the filled buckets back to their huts. To bathe with any privacy at all requires that they slip out late at night and, in the darkness, use the taps in the bustee. For Muslim women, with their concern for modesty, the arrangement is not just inconvenient; it is deeply humiliating.

Under grim conditions you can do nothing about, there is something inhibiting, even indecent, about peeking into other people's lives. The social welfare organization Unnayan, which works with the squatters, will not take visitors into the settlement, for it might jeopardize their credibility as a trusted link with the outside. But unwillingness to look closely at poverty and to imagine what life must be like in such deprivation would be callous and insensitive. If there is an element of voyeurism here, at least it is for a good purpose.

When you ask why the problem of squatting cannot be resolved, why at least the rudimentary necessities for hygiene cannot be provided, the standard answer you get is that the problem arises in the countryside. The *panchayat,* or council system of local government, in the rural areas, along with flood control and improved relief operations, have helped to slow down migration. Even so, dispossessed peasants and landless laborers stream into the city looking for work. To make conditions in Calcutta better for migrants will only encourage more of this in-migration. Why not at least legalize those settlements which are not creating any serious obstruction or public health risk? The response to this is that the squatters would sell their titles, take the cash, and put up illegal shelters somewhere else. Because of this vicious circle, the argument goes, the problem will never go away. It must be acknowledged that in some squatter settlements some basic services are being provided. But in most, as can be easily seen from the roadside (even without looking too closely), conditions remain as awful as ever.

City awakening

Street children

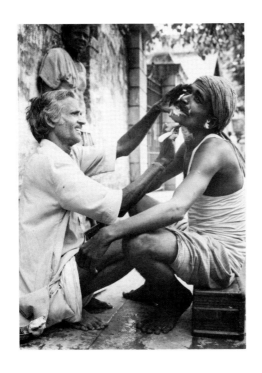

Sidewalk barber

At the water tap

Pavement-dwelling family

Squatter settlement along the canal

Sidewalk shelters

Rail colony with kothabari behind it

Waiting for a job

Scavenging

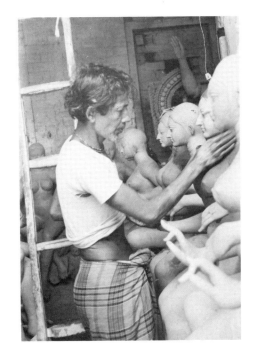

Kumartuli image maker

Khatal

Bustee courtyard

Bustee cricket game

Crumbling elegance

Bihari rickshaw puller

Bustees from Within

The bustees first grew up in residential areas where the Bengali elite made land available so that poor people, especially those who did work for them, could build their mud huts and pay a nominal rent. There was no systematic planning or infrastructure because, as far as the landowners were concerned, they were only renting out bare land. The bustees were seen as temporary abodes for persons who had not made a permanent commitment to town life, and it was expected that they would gradually give way to proper town development.

Often someone would rent a parcel of land on which to build huts to rent out to immigrants, using part of the rent to compensate the landowner. These intermediary developers of the land were known as *thika* tenants, which literally means "temporary tenants," a obvious misnomer when they and their descendants continued to exercise control over certain bustee holdings for generations.

Most bustees were set up in poorly drained sites around ponds and earthen reservoirs, known as "tanks," created by the excavations of hut builders gathering soil for construction or draining off pools and swampy areas. Before unfiltered piped water was extended to these areas beginning in the 1880s, these tanks were the main source of water. Often the only open space in a congested bustee where people gathered to bathe and wash their clothes, the tank also served the social functions of a village well. Circulation within the bustee was more of the village pattern, with narrow meandering lanes between the closely packed huts. For each group of huts, "service privies" were provided to collect human excreta in earthen or tin vessels to be removed manually.

With the rapid growth of commercial and industrial activity in the second half of the nineteenth century, new bustees were built near the port or close to factory sites along the riverfront to provide cheap accommodation for workers. Many of the thirty-five municipalities bordering the Hooghly grew up on a spot where a jute mill was built, with a bustee nearby for the workers later developing into a township which, over time, fused with neighboring townships into a single metropolitan area.

A landlord or factory owner would lease out property to a thika tenant, who built lines of huts separated by narrow lanes with drains down the middle. These he would rent out to migrants, preferably people from his own community or caste. In his dual capacity as landlord and *sardar*—headman or labor supervisor—his authority might include the recruitment of workers and allotment of jobs on behalf of the mill owner. In return for making these arrangements, he was paid a lump or recurring sum by the workers. And should they need some money to visit their families in the village, he could make some short-term credit available. The system was inherently corrupt, and its oppressiveness would have been absolute had it not been for the underlying kinship and community relationships, which ensured an element of reciprocity. These thika tenants and headmen, we learn, sometimes built temples and mosques for the workers under them.

Probably every large property owner of Calcutta owned some bustee land. This is not to suggest that all members of the bhadralok elite were well off. Among them were Hindu widows who were not allowed to dispose of their land but lacked capital to invest in improvements. "Many holdings were jointly owned under Hindu family law, and in such cases it was often very difficult, sometimes impossible, to get agreement on improvements. . . . Many bustee owners lived hand-to-mouth on rents received."[47]

Bustee hutments were built of mud-packed bamboo walls and roofed at first with straw and later with burnt clay tiles. Subdivided into small cubicles, they were grouped around small courtyards accessible from unpaved lanes and bylanes. This is still the typical configuration: a tight clustering of huts separated by narrow lanes three to five feet wide. Conditions were considerably improved with the installation of paved footpaths, drains, sanitary latrines, and drinking water taps. Still, drainage was often blocked, latrines and water taps used by too many people, and garbage not properly disposed of. For thirty or more persons to use one latrine or water tap was nothing exceptional. Muddy lanes were flooded in the slightest rains, and during the monsoons they could remain inundated with drain and sewer water for days. Lighting was often inadequate, and there was little air circulation both within the houses and in the bustee as a whole.

Officially, a bustee was any collection of huts standing on a plot of land not less than ten cottahs in area, or about one-sixth of an acre. The huts were described by legislation as any building of which no substantial part was constructed of "masonry, reinforced concrete, steel, iron or other metal." According to a survey in the late 1950s before any major effort was undertaken to improve the bustees, the average size of registered holdings was half an acre and contained eight to ten hutments, each of which would be shared by at least six families, for an average of four occupants per room. Rooms were also used for petty manufacturing and trading purposes. Since then, densities have further increased, the average number of persons per room being 4.5 persons at the time of the 1981 census. Some cubicles have a separate kitchen, but in one-room huts, the kitchen is in a corner of the room.

The findings from official surveys pertain to the registered bustees and not those on plots of less than the prescribed minimum area. At the time of inheritance a thika tenant's property might be subdivided into units of less than ten cottahs, and there have undoubtedly been cases of subdivision as a means of escaping registration. Consequently, throughout the city are found miniscule pockets of unregistered bustees, which are more or less similar to the clusters of shacks put up here and there by squatters. Precise legal distinctions do not necessarily accord with reality, and statistics as reported in surveys and censuses must be treated with caution.

Nor can statistics portray the day-to-day living conditions in a bustee: the absence of ventilation and sunlight, the tedium of standing in long queues to obtain water or to use the municipal latrine, no separate bath even for women, no school or place where children can play, open drains running down the middle of each lane where people sit, cooking at open fires, buying and selling at tiny stalls—"a housing hell, the like of which is seldom to be found in the vast open rural areas of the country."[48]

Calcutta was the largest metropolis in India up until 1981, when it was overtaken by Bombay. The total population at that time was 10.2 million, of which 3.7 million were said to live in bustees, refugee colonies, and squatter settlements and another million or more in decrepit multistory apartment blocks. Central Calcutta, as distinct from the metropolitan area, sprawls for 50 miles along both sides of the Hooghly and is under the jurisdiction of the Calcutta Metropolitan Corporation (CMC). Its total population in 1991 numbered 4.4 million in a 72-square-mile area. In each of its 141 wards are found from as few as two to as many as 65 bustees, in which apparently some 1.8 million persons live, or just over 40 percent of the total CMC population (see map, opposite page).

Surveys done in 1980 and 1990 showed that important changes were taking place. The joint family pattern was on the wane. There were fewer infants living in the bustees than in the past, probably due to the increased prevalence of nuclear families as well as the availability of more effective family planning services.

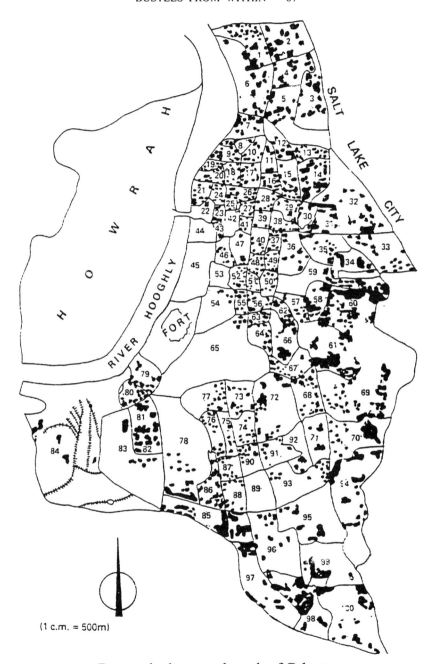

Bustees in the central wards of Calcutta

There were more bustee dwellers who were literate or had a primary education, and there was more female employment. These improvements in literacy and levels of education, especially that of females, suggested that education programs were gradually having an impact. Incomes, duly adjusted for consumer price index changes, seemed also to be improving somewhat. At least, the percentage of households in the lowest earning category declined over the ten-year period.[49]

It was also found that the overall bustee population was remaining quite stable. Forty percent of households had lived in the bustees for more than one generation, and 60 percent were present-generation migrants. When those who had left family members behind in their villages became old and returned home, sons and nephews would replace them in the bustee. In short, households continued to exist even as their composition underwent change. In the Bengali-speaking bustees where whole families had migrated from their rural homes, the male-female distribution was more balanced, as would be expected.

The surveys also showed a wide range of skills and vocations. Out of all income earners, 30 percent were casual laborers; 25 percent had administrative and clerical jobs; 21 percent were shopkeepers, shop assistants, salesmen, and hawkers; 10 percent were teachers, nurses, medical practitioners, lawyers, sculptors, painters, and photographers; 8 percent were in food and beverage processing, tailoring, carpentry, hosiery, production of small engineering items, electrical fittings, blacksmithing, tool making, jewelry, printing; and 6 percent in marginal occupations other than ragpicking and begging, which ranged from paper bag making to painting, from shoe shining to the priesthood. Put simply, the bustees were no haven exclusively for the down-and-out by any stretch of the imagination.

Only 11 percent of income earners were females, mainly in domestic service, which is also considered to be a marginal vocation, being irregular and extremely poorly paid. Most women were housewives. No doubt in a bustee just to survive and to care for children were, in themselves, a full-time job.

Income data were harder to come by. Men became suspicious when asked how much they made, and women usually did not know the income of their husbands. Reported amounts ranged from 500 to 2,000 rupees a month, the average being 1,300 rupees, which translated at the time into about $50. Almost 70 percent of average earnings was being spent on food.

What the surveys did not reveal were the sharp differences between one bustee and the next with regard to occupations, per capita incomes, caloric intake, and other measures of poverty. Therefore, aggregated data of a statistical nature need to be supplemented with findings from visits to homes in different bustees. Interviews recently conducted by women in 34 bustees to obtain data on health and nutrition provide an unsparing depiction of details without the emotional overlay that often colors descriptions of slums. Every gradation of conditions is found:[50]

In a Muslim bustee, the family of one interviewee consists of herself, her husband, and her one-year-old son, living in a single room 17 feet by 12 feet, which they share with two other families, making a total of eight persons in the one room (in addition to the hens running about). Each family has its own hearth. During a heavy shower, the room becomes waterlogged and only dries out after two or three days.

In a Hindu, Bengali-speaking bustee where some refugees from East Bengal have lived for thirty years, houses are still predominantly made of bamboo and mats with flat tile roofs. A number of families have built small bathrooms with mats and gunny sacking. Most family members bathe and wash their clothes in a nearby pond. Garbage is dumped in a open area near the community latrine, which has nine seats for a total population of 910 persons. Only the small children do not use the latrine, defecating instead on a piece of paper, which is then thrown into the open areas used for garbage. After cleaning up the child, the mother cleans her hands with ash and mud, which is also used for cleaning utensils.

In one of the oldest bustees in the city, centrally located and inhabited almost entirely by Hindi- and Urdu-speaking Muslims, most houses are pucca but seriously overcrowded. Those who own their houses have illegally added a second and third floor to accommodate additional family members resulting from the natural increase of population by marriage. Community solidarity among Muslims is strong, and after getting married, the male members prefer to settle in the same bustee, however overcrowded conditions may be. A number of households share a common lane, where they kindle their chulas (although some use kerosene stoves). Without windows and ventilation, the rooms get dark and full of smoke produced in the adjacent households.

In a mainly Bengali-speaking Hindu bustee, the conditions are much better: brick masonry walls and flat tiled roofs, no shortage of water. Sweepers from the municipality collect garbage regularly and clean the roads. All the earlier dry latrines have been converted into sewer-connected latrines. The only serious problem is flooding during the rainy season when the chula must be placed on the bed or on a stool. Also, a nearby plastic factory fills some of the houses with gas, and the windows are too small for ventilation.

Often a bustee will be surrounded by small manufacturing and repair shops. Even within the bustee, rooms will be rented out as shops, godowns, hotels, garages, and temples. Workshops churn out a bewildering array of dyes, chemicals, paints, rubber products, recycled plastic, furniture, laminations, printed circuit boards, ceramic ware. These are the microenterprises of the informal sector that have always been encouraged by government because they create jobs for the slum population. There is a price to pay, however. The obsolescent equipment pumps out smoke, toxic waste, and noxious fumes. The relentless hammering, sawing, forging, welding, vulcanizing, printing, and burning fill the bustee night and day with noise and pollution.

It becomes clear from walking through the slum neighborhoods of Calcutta that no two bustees are the same. Visit any two bustees and you see differences which transcend simple levels of physical amenities: both are densely crowded but one appears orderly, reasonably clean, and well maintained, while the other seems squalid and hopeless. In one, the stamped clay floor of the small courtyard is carefully swept. Inside each of the cubicles which surround the courtyard, the floor is wiped clean, a calendar and religious decorations adorn the walls, cups and saucers are carefully stacked on small shelves, the bed is raised on stands of bricks (again, so the children can sleep underneath), in the corner a small stove and some aluminum pots for cooking are emphatically clean, and at the entrance to the small interior courtyard, there is a water tap and washing bowl on a pedestal and a small Hindu altar. In the other bustee, families live on a common lane, the garbage lies uncollected, latrines are uncovered, and water is obtained from a tap that only intermittently functions. A sludge-covered tank or canal is used for washing and bathing, or the women wash their utensils with mud and ash within their bedrooms.

The differences stem in part from what is regarded as public and what is private. Typically dwellings are clean and tidy inside, even though they are seriously overcrowded. Outside, however, the garbage and refuse from homes and workshops is dumped not in designated spots or at designated times, but everywhere and at any time along the streets and lanes.

Visit a poor neighborhood on a religious holiday, when the gods and the goddesses are dragged out, and there is brief escape from reality. Go, for example, to a Hindu area during Durga Puja, when everyone gathers before the pandal, when worshippers make their offerings of flowers and children delight in the colorful images, the beating of drums, and the music blaring from loudspeakers well above the lawful decibel level, or during Holi, the springtime festival of renewal and cheer, when friends rub red powder on each other's faces for good luck, and strangers douse one another with colored water. Or go to a Muslim area during the Id-ul-Fitr at the end of the month of fasting, when a perceptible vitality fills the air; the men in their spotlessly white kurtas embracing each other and exchanging befitting salutations, the women in sparkling fresh saris, with silver bangles and anklets, the children in spangled clothes, with jeweled studs affixed to earlobes and noses, and rings on fingers and toes. Here the ice cream and sweetmeat vendors carry on a thriving business, a primitive merry-go-round spins to the delight of its riders, while some monkeys and perhaps even an evidently miserable black bear chained by the nose, matted hair covered with dust, are brought out to perform for some rupees. For the visitor, a community spirit and overwhelming feeling of joy seem to eclipse the normal drab physical stereotype of what living in a bustee is like.

There are some bustees, however, that lack *samaj*, or a sense of community (which, it is said, stems from the custom of caste members eating together on festive and religious occasions). In a Bengali bustee on the south side of Calcutta, different groups competed against each other to raise contributions for important pujas rather than cooperating and organizing a more impressive festival which would do credit to the community as a whole. Urged to form a development committee, the people were reluctant to contribute "even a meagre four annas monthly" to keep the roads and drains clean. The prevailing psychic and social disorganization permeated the lives of families, as seen in the weakening of family and kinship relations when both spouses were working. For lack of space within the hut, leisure time was spent outside, at the cost of intimate familial relationships. Husband and wife did not pool their earnings. The husband spent his extra money loitering in the tea shop, smoking hemp, playing cards with friends. With their parents away much of the time, older siblings had to look after their brothers and sisters, bring water from the pump, and do the cooking. Boys as young as eight began to stay away from home, and by age twelve, boys and girls started working as day laborers or as maidservants in the neighboring kothabari. The usual conventions and norms of respect to parents and relatives were absent. Because of paucity of space for entertaining, contact with kin, even with those living nearby, was kept to a minimum. If kin lived in the kothabari and were regarded as babu, there was further separation in terms of education and general behavior. Participation in weddings and other important family ceremonies became rare, and relatives lost contact with each other. In any case, there was no place in the home to put up a relative visiting from some distance away.[51]

A quite different picture was drawn in the case of a low-caste, Hindi-speaking community of sweepers (the workers who remove night soil and other filth) where, despite poverty, ceremonies and social functions are accorded much importance. The general apathy of the higher-caste, Bengali-speaking Hindu society living in the pucca apartments around them and the bustee dwellers' strong ties with their home villages induced them to develop a strong in-group sentiment. They organized a club which ran a night school and a free dispensary and had a small library. In "following the babu way of life," the club sought to remove the evils of slum life, such as drinking country liquor and gambling. There also interpersonal disputes were settled. Neighbors from the surrounding apartments never went into the bustee, and babu boys did not mix with the slum kids. For their part, the bustee dwellers did not actively try to establish closer relationships with the surrounding community. Rather, they sought to improve the image of the bustee and mitigate discrepancies with the wider metropolitan culture. Residents expressed a positive outlook on their life, which was better than before.

> Our business is to remove filth. After this duty, when we return to our house we never touch anybody or go inside a room without taking a bath. . . . But after that we have liberty to go anywhere we like. Nobody bothers about our caste. We can even take tea from the tea-stall situated at the main road along with the higher-caste babus. Don't think that the babus cannot recognize us. Here we do not have restrictions. But in our villages it does not matter whether you remove filth or not; if you are once recognized as a Hela [low-caste] nobody will touch you. If you wear a clean dress they will taunt you. You will get tea in earthen pots instead of a glass or a cup. That's why we prefer to live in Calcutta.[52]

Then there is another bustee which includes both Muslims and Hindus, living in a sort of delicate equilibrium. The pattern of settlement is along religious lines. Hindu activity centers around the Kali temple, Muslim around the mosque. In both communities, however, slum life is attuned with the rural life, where the people return at regular intervals to their home villages to work on their land, and on social and religious occasions. Muslims and Hindus know each other well, their children play together. They play cards, chat, exchange *biris,* and joke with each other. There is mutual help across religious lines. But despite this appearance of harmony, communal antagonism may surface from time to time, and it was here that large-scale violence erupted at the time of independence.[53] For that matter, any insult to the honor of the religious community will provoke strong and collective reactions: the playing of music by Hindu religious processions in front of mosques, for example, or throwing red water on a Muslim during Holi.

The same overall picture was true in Pilkhana (a.k.a. Anand Nagar or City of Joy), a very large bustee in Howrah, which was described in its raw state in Dominique Lapierre's book *City of Joy* before any bustee improvement took place. Residents were mainly Muslims but also included Hindus and small numbers of Sikhs, Jains, Christians, and Buddhists. Despite overcrowding and excruciating poverty, they "shared in a communal world and respected its social and religious values, maintaining the ancestral traditions and beliefs." Lapierre told of how Hindu women assisted their Muslim neighbors with the cooking of traditional feasts or brought saffron and henna to embellish their friends faces, arms, and feet, and how Muslims took Hindus into their homes when the whole area was flooded by the monsoon.[54]

Improving the Bustees

In the early years of Calcutta, the bustees were seen as a passing phenomenon, a blot on the landscape that would, in time, go away. Bustee residents were regarded as inferior, uncivilized, and best ignored. The 1870s, however, witnessed mounting popular concern regarding such living conditions—not out of any solicitude for the suffering inhabitants but rather out of fear that the bustee might become a breeding ground for diseases that could threaten the town as a whole. Some of the infamous "tanks" (earthern reservoirs) around which bustee huts clung were filled in an effort to clean up the sites. Street sweepings were used as fill because Calcutta was short of soil, until doubts were raised about this practice when it was learned that mysterious gases were being produced. A health officer told of a woman who had not been able to extinguish her cooking fire, which had burned continually for several weeks, causing marvel and fear among the bustee dwellers, to whom it was "the tongue and the breath of the devil."[55] Of more general concern at the time was that filling in tanks only contributed to greater congestion as more huts were built on the former tank sites.

Improving bustees entailed opening up roads even if it meant that residents had to move elsewhere. There are reports of entire bustees being cleared for the construction of materials depots and tramway company stables. Some of the open ditches were sewered, filled in, and converted into paths, but generally they were too narrow and winding to permit any real improvement. Not until the end of the nineteenth century were new bustees required to adhere to specific house alignments and minimum separation.

Sometimes owners of bustees would pull down the huts and replace them with two- and three-story masonry buildings. These early instances of upgrading were done with little regard for drainage or that the only access was via narrow and winding passages. Even less concern was given to the hardships inflicted on the residents who were displaced. The municipality itself, for that matter, was in the redevelopment business. We learn that in 1858, for instance, it acquired a plot of land crowded by huts occupied by domestic servants and native livery stables that were considered to be "a great nuisance to the residents within the immediate vicinity." The municipality excavated a tank to provide a good supply of "wholesome water fit for drinking and sold the surplus land, on condition that it be used to build houses which could be rented at not less than 100 rupees per month."[56]

Removing waste from bustee land was no easy matter. The bustees were so congested, their lanes so narrow, that the town's conservancy carts could not enter. Nightsoil in those days was removed by private individuals who were paid by the occupants of the premises. Known as *mehtars*—sweepers—they carried "the baskets of filth full of stink" on their heads to special depots, whence the contents were eventually taken to the Nightsoil Ghat, a special landing stair on the Hooghly, to be transported downstream and dumped into the river at ebb tide—that is, when not simply tossed into any nearby tank, pool, or trench under cover of darkness, or scattered to be dried in the sun.[57]

Early efforts at bustee improvement were the responsibility of the municipal corporation, which collected rates directly from the residents—without much conviction or success. The landlords who stood to benefit from the enhanced value of their properties invested nothing whatsoever. The system was therefore changed to require landowners to pay the rates on behalf of the bustee inhabitants, leaving it to them to recover the money. Predictably, the landlords complained, fearing that it would be impossible to recover what they had paid without resorting to tedious civil suits. To this, the chairman of the municipal corporation retorted: "The landlords have literally grown rich in their sleep. Can they, forsooth, complain of injustice?"[58]

Toward the end of the nineteenth century progress had been made in filling in the insanitary tanks, extending conservancy services to the bustees, providing filtered and unfiltered water, and replacing open drains with an underground system. But well into the present century, the disposal of sewage never caught up with the relentless spread of bustees into areas that were much worse off with respect to drainage and water supply. By the mid-1950s Calcutta had earned a reputation of being the "cholera capital of the world," with more than a thousand cholera deaths a year. Called in to make recommendations, the World Health Organization noted in its report:

> A peculiar ecological feature which exerts an ominous influence on the incidence of cholera is the large number of bustee areas in most wards of the city. Here refugees and other under-privileged people are crowded together, nearly or sometimes even altogether bereft of adequate safe water supplies and other proper sanitary conveniences. . . . Two-thirds of the cholera attacks are encountered in the bustee huts. . . .[59]

There were at that time a million persons living in the bustees in the Calcutta Metropolitan Corporation (CMC) area (not to mention those living in Howrah and the adjacent municipalities). Somewhat less than 400,000 were to be found in the more central, sewered areas. A greater number were living on the edge of the city, where the health situation was worse. These outlying areas, where most families used bucket privies, were also worse off in respect to drainage, being low-lying and easily swamped during the rains and covered in places by stagnant ponds or tanks polluted with refuse and sewage. Because of the inadequate supply of safe water, the tanks were used for bathing and for washing clothes and utensils. According to 1962–1963 data, the incidence of cholera in unsewered areas was 9.96 cases per thousand, compared to 7.6 cases per thousand in the sewered bustees.

Throughout history, urban poverty and disease have gone hand in hand. Living malnourished in high-density squalor amid vermin, uncollected waste, and untreated sewage led to epidemics of malaria, dysentery, tuberculosis, typhoid, and typhus, as well as plague and other horrific diseases. The fear that disease emanating from the bustees would contaminate the affluent neighborhoods had provoked some remedial action in the nineteenth century. Now, once again, what alarmed the outside world was not that people were dying in Calcutta but the threat of a more general epidemic. Cholera could easily spread outward along the routes of the two principal railway systems linking Calcutta with the rest of India, and from there to the rest of the world.

How to deal with bustee conditions had been a subject of contention since the turn of the century. Health officers argued that wholesale demolition of the huts was the only solution. Business interests, counting on a plentiful supply of cheap migrant labor, argued that bustees were the most appropriate accommodation for the poor. Pucca houses, they said, "if after the London style of workmen's dwelling or any other style" would not be suitable, owing to the expense. Besides, "the poorer class of people, not being accustomed to anything but their hut dwellings, might have other objections against occupying them."[60] While the debate was going on, the land continued to be cleared wherever bustee huts were too close to European quarters or private property interests were at stake. Any landlord wanting to evict some tenants from his property could do it with the help of the law, often merely by showing that he wanted to build a pucca home.

By the mid-1950s the gradual clearing away of the bustees and the relocation of residents, as envisaged by legislation, proved impracticable because of the prohibitive cost and resistance from the bustee owners. Some private clearance was attempted in the central city. The experience was not encouraging, however. Substantial payments were required to induce occupants to move and not resist on legal grounds. They usually ended up finding shelter in other bustees, which in turn became more congested. By that time also, party activists of the leftist opposition were giving their support to bustee dwellers threatened with eviction or harassment by landlords and the *goondas*, or neighborhood bullies, they hired to vandalize and burn down the huts. Once their consciousness of injustice was aroused, residents became politically mobilized. They met efforts of eviction with determined resistance. A thika tenant in a Baghbazar bustee remembers:

> [The landlord] tried at least three times to evict the bustee people with Court Order and police force. Such threats were resisted by us under the red flag with women and children coming to the forefront. A big gathering of thousands of people formed when they came to evict. It became obvious if the police went ahead with their clearing there would be bloodshed. . . .[61]

Carrying out any bustee improvement was complicated by the three-tier tenancy system which prevailed in Calcutta: the land belonging to one person, the huts to another, and the occupant paying a monthly rent without any claim to the land or to the hut. Because bustees were on private land, the city renounced any responsibility. Landowners spent next to nothing on their properties and were unwilling to invest in improvements, expecting high returns if their unimproved properties could be sold on the open market. Under no circumstances were they prepared to support improvements which would serve to consolidate the existing occupancy arrangements. Nor did the well-being of the bustee dwellers really concern them; being typically absentee, landowners had little to do with their tenants.

The legal position of the thika tenants, who had put up the huts on the land and usually lived in the bustees themselves, was different. They were secure because legislation soon after Indian independence had given them protection against eviction by landlords. As far as they were concerned, any improvement scheme was acceptable provided it confirmed their continued tenancies and the uninterrupted flow of their rental income. Although later permitted to make huts pucca, they had little incentive to do so because of rent controls and because they had no proprietary rights to the land. Thus, from their different perspectives, neither landlords nor hut owners were staunchly supportive of improving conditions. From a government standpoint, protecting the interests of the some 30,000 hut-owning middlemen (with their formidable political clout) while at the same time safeguarding the tenancy rights of bustee dwellers prevented any definitive solution.

Further complicating matters is the fact that bustees have never been entirely synonymous with poverty. People do not always live there because they are poor. Forty percent of households have regular wage-paying jobs and earn incomes above the poverty line (which is defined in terms of the monetary equivalent of a basic nutritional requirement of 2,100 calories per person per day). It is not surprising to find businessmen living in a bustee alongside sweepers and unskilled laborers. Entry of persons into the lowest-income housing market, even though they can afford better accommodations, tends to price out the poorer residents, pushing them into homelessness and squatter conditions.

Such self-imposed poverty can be explained in the context of migrant attitudes. Their stay in the city, no matter how long, is regarded as temporary. Because their objective is to earn money, not to set up a home, they willingly accept substandard accommodations. Even if they could afford a better place to live, bustees allow them to keep housing expenses to a minimum. Extreme instances of this are the three-shift sleeping arrangements common in the coolie lines of the jute mills.

A comprehensive urban development plan, drawn up with assistance from the Ford Foundation, was issued in 1966. Unlike most orthodox plans, this Basic Development Plan, as it was called, did not include a master land-use plan or vision of the future. Rather, it proposed urgent actions to be undertaken within the framework of a flexible, twenty-year plan, including three new towns, two urban renewal projects, a long-term shelter program involving slum improvements, over 200,000 primary and secondary school places, community services and facilities, open spaces, a metropolitan transportation program, and the creation of a structure of public institutions for implementing the plan. Most of the financing went into water supply, sanitation and drainage, and transportation. Probably the most significant achievement of the plan, however, in the eyes of many of those directly involved, was the Bustee Improvement Program (BIP).

The development plan dealt with the whole of the metropolitan district and with a diverse array of services and infrastructure. There was no single agency equipped to implement its proposals. The metropolitan district was governed by a patchwork of municipalities, city corporations, specialized authorities, and improvement trusts. Some influential political leaders were stubbornly opposed to the creation of a centralized metropolitan agency to oversee implementation of the plan. However, the accelerating decay of the city during a period of political turbulence and the need to put people to work on long-delayed projects necessitated the creation of the Calcutta Metropolitan Development Authority (CMDA), which was given an open license to get going on the reconstruction of the city.

The plan presented the need for undertaking a massive program to improve the bustees. What struck the planners most sharply was the economic incapacity of government to clear thousands of bustee holdings in which some two million people lived and to rehouse those people. As Arthur Row, a Ford Foundation consultant, wrote in his later evaluation of the program:

> It took courage, particularly on the part of the Indian staff, to propose a program of simple environmental improvement, acknowledging that for most of the bustee dwellers the bustees would be their homes for years and decades to come. The planners also recognized that, coincident with physical improvement, there should be programs for social and economic improvement in the lives of the bustee people.

Although this conclusion was being reached elsewhere in the 1960s . . .
political attitudes in India were governed by middle-class norms, and
gaining acceptance of [this] point of view in the face of both bureaucratic and political opposition was no mean feat.[62]

From sorry experience, CMDA recognized the impossibility of
dealing with the housing problem through redevelopment and
infill projects. In the fifties and sixties some four- and five-story
walk-ups had been built on land cleared of huts, with surplus
land sold off to pay for construction. But even after the sale of
land, the per capita cost of rehousing turned out to be excessive.
Rents had to be heavily subsidized to remain within the capacity
of many of the bustee dwellers, and there were problems of
maintenance. Although given some compensation, thika tenants
were opposed to these schemes under which they lost the rents
they had received as hut owners and became simple tenants like
the rest.

Trying this approach in one bustee (in the Chetla area) in the
early seventies, CMDA had to contend with lengthy litigation,
clearing over forty court cases before it could complete the project, which even today wears an abandoned look. Bitter feelings
led to violence. The minister in charge at that time was injured at
a ceremony for the allocation of new apartments. Residents were
unaccustomed to multistory living and the loss of ground space
so important for their lifestyle and economic activities. They did,
however, like the common toilet and shower facilities, which
were cleaner and more accessible than those in the bustee.

With the Slum Areas (Clearance and Improvement) Act of
1971, emphasis shifted from redevelopment to improvement of
housing units already in place. The government was given ease-
ment rights to acquire land and rights-of-way for improvements
without paying compensation. Issues of tenure and the need to
finance housing were avoided. Attention was focused instead on
basic sanitation and environmental upgrading: one water tap per
hutment or per one hundred persons, "sanitary latrines" with septic tank or sewer connections to replace manually cleaned bucket

privies, surface drainage, paving of roads and pathways, and provision of security lighting, garbage bins, bathing-cum-washing
platforms, and "tot lots" for children. With World Bank financing, the program was initially designed to provide these basic
services to one million slum dwellers at an average cost of one
hundred rupees per head (or about $14 at the time).

It was important to infringe as little as possible on the rights
and interests of landowners and hut owners. This respect for the
status quo precluded undertaking a more comprehensive program, and now, twenty years later, the dilapidated state of many
of the "improved" bustees is a source of criticism. Standards of
sanitation remain fairly low, and some of the bustees are still ill
ventilated, unhygienic, and poorly lit. Being short-term and remedial in nature, the modest improvements in infrastructure that
were made did not satisfy longer-term expectations. It was simply too difficult politically to dispossess thika tenants of their
properties (with compensation) and invest hut ownership in the
actual occupants; in short, to provide real security of tenure.
Given the stratified tenurial system, a limited program of environmental upgrading, whatever its deficiencies, was the only fea-
sible way to go about improving the bustees.

In the meantime, occupancy rates were mounting. Some thika
tenants showed no qualms in exploiting their tenants and behav-
ing as true slumlords; they subdivided unremittingly to get as
much rent as possible. This put greater strain on the infrastructure
that had been installed. Hut occupants, moreover, were negligent
in maintaining facilities which were being used by large numbers
of people. Sometimes a group of households would engage part-
time sweepers to clean the drains. More likely, they waited for
the municipality to do it. Everything outside their dwellings was
beyond their control, at least beyond that of the individual families. Even where there were conveniently located garbage bins,
refuse was tossed out the door without so much as a second
thought.

The helter-skelter configuration of densely packed huts complicated the laying down of sewer and water lines. Little could be

done to realign huts in order to facilitate installation. In some parts of the city, the septic tanks in the improved bustees could not be connected to the main sewers because of the irregular levels in the hundreds of lanes, or the people could not afford or were unwilling to connect their toilets to the main sewers. So the sewage treatment plant remained, as the CMDA sociologist put it, "an unused monument . . . and many of the slum toilets, built hastily, have become unusable, thereby letting loose the traditional Indian culture to 'flourish' [defecating in the open spaces] . . . and inviting germs and flies for a 'free-for-all.' . . ."[63]

Contending with slum conditions has been further complicated by the many cows and buffalo that are kept in the bustees. The cowsheds, known as *khatals,* are another breeding ground for flies and disease, and, as a former secretary of CMDA pointed out, it is not possible to sustain a sewer network that can service cattle as well. The owners, as politically powerful thika tenants, insist on keeping their cattle close to their customers in the bustees and nearby upper- and middle-class neighborhoods. The milk is sold mainly to families outside, while the manure is used by bustee households for fuel. When efforts are made to remove the cattle, khatal owners go to court, which usually decides in their favor. Schemes to remove many of the 2,200 unhygienic cattle sheds to special colonies on the city's outer fringes have invariably met with strong resistance. Owners refuse to have their cattle relocated because of the high costs of ferrying milk from these centers to their networks of customers in the city. So their khatals, and the flies that go with them, remain a ubiquitous feature of the bustees, as they have for more than two hundred years.

To deal more effectively in upgrading the bustees, the government realized that it had to gain control over the land. Such was the intent of the Thika Tenancy (Acquisition and Regulation) Act of 1981, which aimed at abolishing the three-tier tenancy system. Vesting all bustee land in the state would free residents from the property control of thika tenants and absentee landlords. With the revenues collected from hut owners, the municipality would maintain basic services. Hut owners would be allowed to convert units into multi-storied buildings and accommodate additional tenants. Landlords would be compensated for the loss of future income. Because default in land rent payment was a common experience for them, the provision of even modest compensation would be better than nothing.

Under this legislation, every thika tenant would pay to the state a land rent not less than what he or she (26 percent of thika tenancies were owned by women, at least in name) had been paying to the landlord. The tenants rights could be inherited but not transferred. However, four years after the law went into effect only 10 percent of the estimated 30,000 thika tenants had registered and paid rent. This was explained in part by the fact that many of them reside in the hutment with their families while at the same time renting out a number of rooms to others. Also, many of the holdings under thika arrangements were less than the minimum of ten cottahs in area which legally defines a bustee.[64]

The experience in north Calcutta of the Ramakrishna Mission (a charitable organization which runs schools, hospitals, orphanages, and libraries throughout India) confirms the importance of having urban land under city control. The Rambagan bustee was occupied mainly by Harijan (untouchable) artisan families who earned their living from traditional handicraft work in bamboo, cane, and paper and as artists and musicians. There were also a number of brothels nearby, and except for the coming and going of their patrons, the bustee remained isolated from the surrounding apartment buildings and the city at large.

In the early 1950s, changes began taking place. Middle-class students from a nearby Ramakrishna hostel organized adult literacy classes in the bustee. A social welfare center was set up and began regular classes and vocational training. Health and other services were added later, bringing child mortality rates down sharply. The community began to organize. A people's welfare committee was formed, with subcommittees to deal with health matters, sports, pujas, and theatrical performances. But it was soon realized that these various programs, though critical in energizing the community, would have little sustained impact unless something fundamental was done to improve the deplorable housing conditions.

Under the 1981 legislation, the government conveyed legal title to the land to the Ramakrishna Mission as custodian. The mission, together with the local committee, began a process of progressively buying out the thika tenants, clearing the bustees, and building in their place four-story walk-ups, each with sixteen units composed of two rooms, bath, and a small balcony for cooking. The bustee dwellers contributed fifty paisa to one rupee daily per family to help meet the cost of compensating the thika tenants. Once a walk-up was completed, more huts were demolished and the families moved in.

In the past, the bhadralok families in the neighboring apartments looked down, figuratively and literally, upon the tiled roofs and squalid pathways of the Rambagan bustee. The situation has now been reversed. The new apartment blocks of the bustee stand in fresh contrast to the sadly deteriorated buildings outside. There are TV antennas on the roofs, families socializing and cooking their meals on their balconies, and, in general, more contact between the residents of the neighborhood as a whole despite caste differences. There is even some intermarriage.

Elsewhere, thika tenants have become landlords and hut occupants tenants. With government permission, thika landlords may add floors to their properties. This requires, first, a building plan, which, given building restrictions, is no easy matter in tightly congested areas. Then there is the drawn-out process of obtaining official approval, plus all the intermediate hurdles of fees, payoffs, and kickbacks which this entails. So, more often than not, construction begins without explicit official authorization. The municipal corporation may then see fit to issue a stop work order—which is seldom enforced. The ruling political party does not want to disgruntle its bustee constituency. Official orders are issued but without much conviction or follow-up. Promoters keep on building willy-nilly, and the police are given bribes to look the other way. Once the building is occupied, it is all the more difficult to demolish it. As described in an official report, the results can sometimes be disastrous:

> In the early hours of 28 February 1991, a building at premises No. 8 Collin Lane in Ward No. 63 of the Calcutta Municipal Corporation, in the Park Street Police Station area, collapsed killing many people and injuring many residing in the adjacent premises. This is not the first incident of collapse of a new building or a building under construction. . . .

The report of the investigation went on to point out that the building inspector, in the course of his usual rounds, could not detect the unauthorized construction. Access to the site was too narrow, and some huts protruded on the lane, obstructing his vision from the main road. A month prior to the collapse, a guard was posted to prevent any further construction, but construction continued during the night. A fourth and fifth story were added and plastering begun. A round-the-clock police posting was then ordered by the deputy municipal commissioner, with instructions to arrest the offender in the event of any further violation. Two days prior to the collapse, the police commissioner reported that "local police went to the spot on 20 January 1991 and found that excepting brick works of some portions, construction of the unauthorized building was almost over. And from 20 January 1991 no further construction was done." After the collapse a month later, the owner of the plot, who was among the injured, was arrested. The other two accused persons, who had entered into contract with him to construct the building, absconded.[65]

Unauthorized and unsafe construction of this sort has become increasingly common in the bustees. An unscrupulous promoter convinces the hut owner to allow him to build, promising the latter an apartment and money. Building is done without regard to regulations and codes and with inadequate foundations and inferior materials. One structure in Bhowanipur, built around and on top of several bustee families, fell down on them. The collapse in Collin Lane resulted in the death of fifty-two people, plus injury to many more. Tenants who had invested what funds they had or could borrow to obtain space in the new building (in some cases as little as sixty square feet) were left not just homeless but destitute, without, at last report, having received any compensation.

When all is said and done, there is little doubt that after two decades of effort, living conditions in the bustees have improved for large numbers of people. There are fewer deaths from water-borne diseases. Sanitary latrines (when they function), water points, and bathing platforms are appreciated by the residents. Sewer and underground drainage have removed the insanitary mess of open ditches. Nutrition centers have been set up, and bread and milk distributed to bustee children. Prenatal care has become available, and there has been improvement in literacy rates. Besides these tangible accomplishments, there has been an infusion among residents of a sense of participation in development activities, "a realization about their deplorable environment and pitiful life-style and an aspiration for better living."[66] In this respect, bustee improvement has allayed the sense of anomie and powerlessness which lies at the roots of poverty. Without question, this has been its principal success.

Bustee improvement may now be looked upon as a thing of the past, however, because it has not effectively dealt with the housing problem. The supply of buildable urban land has been far outpaced by the demand, which has pushed land prices up to abnormal levels. Single-storied pockets face the massive pressures of real estate development. The logic of bustee improvement does not allow evicting slum tenants and dismantling such pockets, even though they represent an inefficient use of valuable urban land. Overcrowding reaches a new high as hut owners squeeze in more tenants and add floors to their holdings: the denser the occupancy, the more the income. When bustees are improved, hut owners can demand higher rents, and *salami*—key money—is now required, where it never was in the past. The magnitude of displacement of the poor is uncertain, yet there is evidence that the more vulnerable residents have been priced out of cheaper accommodation. The problem of the slum environment has thus shifted inexorably to the illegal and unserviced squatter settlements, where former bustee dwellers as well as new migrants must turn to meet their dire need for any place whatsoever to live.

Caste and
Occupational Niches

As the famous Bengali anthropologist Nirmal Kumar Bose liked to point out, Calcutta is not a melting pot. Because there are not enough jobs to go around, he wrote, everyone clings as closely as possible to the occupation with which his caste is identified. Immediate kinsmen, occupational group, and common origin constitute a widening circle of networks which provide the individual with the economic support he needs in the city. Ethnic groups tend to cluster together in their own quarters, and voluntary organizations are ethnically more or less exclusive. In the past, the two main religious communities each favored certain occupations: Hindus became merchants and traders, servants, cow keepers and milk sellers, and dealers in brass and bell metal, precious metals, and stones; Muslims chose to become butchers, masons, boatmen, grooms, and water carriers.

A castelike segregation in residence as well as in occupational preferences has been characteristic of Calcutta from the earliest days. The town was divided into a number of quarters, each allotted to one professional group or caste, and the quarters named after predominant occupations: Kumartuli for the kumar, or potters, Colootola for the kalu, or oil pressers, Jeliatola for the jelia, or fishermen, Goaltooli for the goala, or milkmen, and Domtooli for the dom, or scavengers. Thus, too, the butchers concentrated in Cossaitola, the bell metal workers in Kansaripara, the conch shell workers in Sankaritola, the sweepers in Haripara, the tailors in Darjipara, the dealers in country blankets in Kambulitola, the blacksmiths in Kamarpara, the carpenters in Chootarpara, the painters in Patualtola, the washermen in Dhopapara, and the petty traders in Beparitola. The descendants of the Portuguese, who were the only keepers of fowl *(murgi),* lived in a quarter known as Murghihatta, and Armenian Ghat and Armenian Street still recall the days when the locality was occupied by the Armenian community.[67]

Many Calcutta neighborhoods today retain an ethnic and linguistic homogeneity inherited from the earliest families that settled in the area. This separate identity is expressed in the neighborhood associations and youth clubs that organize sporting events, charities, theatrical presentations, and the performance of collective worship. Its importance to the ordinary citizen is most vividly apparent on the occasion of the important festivals for the Hindu deities when neighborhoods compete in constructing elaborate *pandals,* the platforms made of bamboo and pleated cloth and decorated with chandeliers, in which the sacred images are placed, and in adorning the streets with festive banners and bunting. In the Muslim quarters there is a similar expression of solidarity during the celebration of Id-ul-Fitr, Id-ul-Zuha, Moharram, and the Birthday of the Prophet, in which neighborhood clubs play a key part.

Unlike caste in the traditional sense, the castelike occupations that urban residents take up are not actually ranked into high and low, although some may be regarded as more respectable than others. Trading can be undertaken by almost any caste. The city provides scope for social mobility that was not present in the earlier village society, with its narrower range of occupations and technologies and rigid caste hierarchy. New urban occupations help groups dissociate themselves from their parent castes of lower rank and bring them money and influence.

In the earliest days of Calcutta, the need for brokers and interpreters to mediate between the British and the society at large provided a channel for social mobility. People of lower-caste origin filling these roles became accepted among the traditionally dominant castes by virtue of their newly acquired status and wealth. The norms and values that used to bind rural society began to break down. Urban opportunities proliferated and were exploited to the hilt. Bribery and embezzlement became the order of the day among this new Bengali elite, who seemed to be obsessed in making fortunes as fast as possible and establishing dynasties "that would be regarded as successors to the old Hindu 'maharajas' and 'rajas.' "[68]

One means by which persons of a comparatively ordinary caste who had become wealthy could move up in eminence and respectability was by building a temple or bathing ghat on the riverside, or by conspicuous expenditure during religious festivals and marriage ceremonies. The ability to attract Brahmin priests to officiate at his temple assured the parvenu of the clean status of his new caste.

At one time, agriculture was the only alternative occupation open to the lower castes. With economic developments in the eighteenth and nineteenth centuries, however, other opportunities were created with the expansion of European trade and the increased demand for products of Bengal, such as cotton textiles and sugar, and the inland trade in jute, rice, salt, iron, brass, and bell metal wares. An example of this upward mobility was a group of Teli, an oil-pressing caste, whose transactions with the East India Company opened opportunities for them to become small manufacturers and suppliers of silk and silk textiles, and later traders of salt. They then branched into rice and jute, became moneylenders, and went so far as to change their caste name to conceal their impure extraction. They also invested money to become landholders so they could acquire the status of zamindar, "their greatest ambition." Similarly, a breakaway group of Napit, the barber caste, achieved higher status through the manufacture and sale of sweetmeats, and a subcaste of the Suri, whose occupation was the manufacture and sale of liquor, switched over to the trade in food grains and other commodities and became Saha, a more respectable rank.[69]

Caste occupations necessarily changed along with changes in technologies and tastes. Palanquin bearers were displaced by the electric streetcar. The brass and bell metal workers lost out to enamel and aluminum wares; washermen, at least some of them, to the steam laundries, washing machines, and synthetic fibers too delicate to be handled in the old-fashioned way; milkmen, in part, to the importation of powdered milk; manufacturers of coarse, country-made sugar to the preferred factory-made cane sugar; and conch shell workers to the availability of plastic bangles. It is said that only 13 percent of the Brahmins still follow their traditional occupations as priests, pundits, and cooks, and many of them can be found carrying out all kinds of menial tasks.

As in all cities, occupational niches accommodate migrants from particular ethnic groups and localities. There has always been a regular flow of information on wage rates and conditions of work in Calcutta industries back to the villages. Gradually a network of relationships develops through which kinsmen and later migrants gain access to jobs not otherwise available to them. Client groups form around a big merchant of the same ethnic origin. The migrant finds his first work in the city through a kinsman. It is the sardar coming from the same rural locality who will secure a place for him in the mill or when he is dismissed gets him credit for a while until he finds other work or allocates an area for scavenging if there is nothing else to do. In ill health and bad times the migrant falls back on traditional relationships and coreligionists. There is nothing irrational or simply nostalgic in adhering intensely to these ethnic allegiances.

In some cases, caste is important, notably in occupations considered unclean, such as the tanning of leather, and these have consequently been adopted by migrants belonging to inferior castes. By and large, however, occupational groups are more mean-ingful than caste per se in understanding relationships in the urban society. Caste restrictions are no longer raised, for instance, in the work of servants except in what is still considered the lowest kind of work, the cleaning of bathrooms, which is done by *jamadar,* an occupational group, not a caste. Also, new occupational groups have emerged, such as car cleaners and the *istriwalla,* or ironing men, seen in front of apartment buildings using irons heated by coals, who do not have specific caste antecedents.

The story of Calcutta's poor must therefore be told in terms of these occupational niches, not only because they help to explain how the economy is organized and how services function, but also because work of some kind, however humble, gives mean-ing to their lives and evokes pride. Even begging is spoken of as a profession, and some say that prostitution, although unlaw-ful, does not carry the stigma you would ordinarily expect. The story of Calcutta's poor is also one of how occupational niches and ethnic networks are being strained by the pressures of urbanization.

Hand rickshaws first entered passenger service in Calcutta in 1914, then owned by Chinese. Today there may be 35,000 hand rickshaws in the city providing employment for 70,000 to 80,000 pullers,[70] mostly Biharis (whereas bicycle rickshaws, excluded from the central business district, are operated only in the suburbs, mainly by Bengalis). Most of the Biharis who pull rickshaws through the teeming streets and lanes of central and north Cal-cutta leave their families in their home villages, where they re-turn for a part of each year. Often ten or even twenty pullers will rent a common kitchen and room in which to store their belong-ings as well as to serve as identification for a license and dealing with the police. Sleeping accommodations are commonly the sidewalks, but some owners provide sleeping space in the rick-shaw sheds. The vehicle is normally rented from a fleet owner on a shift basis. If it is unlicensed, as a great many of them are, the rickshaw wallah has other costs, such as loss of earnings when his vehicle is impounded, or a bribe to the police of a rupee a day to prevent that from happening. These small payments for immunity from arrest or harassment are the norm.

Rickshaws have many advantages. They are available day and night. They penetrate the narrow lanes as no other public transport can. They are comfortable compared to a crowded bus or streetcar. Women can get about in them in relative seclusion. A regularly used puller provides a safe way to send children to school. When streets are flooded rickshaws become indispensable.

Popular perceptions about rickshaws, however, differ sharply. In the view of some, such as the taxi driver who rages at the stick-thin rickshaw wallah, straining on his shafts, for not giving way quick enough, they are an anachronism which should be swept away with obsolescence of all sorts. To others, they are a quintessential part of Calcutta's heritage despite its imperfections, to which rickshaws are attuned. Predictably, traffic policy accords priority to mass transit needs served by buses and streetcars, not to rickshaws, nor for that matter to the pedestrians, who take their lives in their hands every time they cross a Calcutta street, or the hawkers, who depend upon the streets for their subsistence. A move is even currently afoot in the state government to abolish rickshaws altogether, the argument being that pulling them is an "inhuman job," besides giving a bad impression of the city. Before that can happen, however, as proponents themselves will admit, some alternative employment would have to be found for the thousands of pullers who would be displaced.

Most of the inorganic waste, such as paper, rags, metals, and glass, is picked by scavengers from the large vats or garbage bins strategically located throughout the city. Rags are used for papermaking, metals for resmelting, broken glass for remelting, and plastics are recycled too. Their poverty induces scavengers, or ragpickers as they are locally known, to collect cinders—fragments of half-burned coal—which they wash and dry before selling, and green coconut shells, which are used as cheap fuel. They cannot sell damp paper or very dirty plastic, so they must first take it home and dry it for a day or two.

When the vats are emptied and their contents taken to the municipal garbage dumps, you would expect that there would be nothing left of value worth recovering. Surprisingly, however, the Dhapa dump area on the eastern edge of the city is put to productive use by some 100,000 individuals, who process whatever waste is still recyclable. They belong to a number of separate caste and tribal groups which undertake impure work of this nature and regulate their range of activities through caste-based conventions. Some of them use organic waste to grow vegetables on "garbage farms," which produce cauliflower, gourds, and corn. Up to 25,000 of them pick and sort garbage from the ever-mounting dumps. For this "privilege" they pay regular fees to dump managers and truck drivers and organize themselves to parcel out picking territories. About the same number are engaged in skinning carcasses, tanning skins and hides, shaving wool and hair, while another 10,000 or more are employed in retrieving "offal, dead flesh, bones, and hoofs which are converted into a large variety of products: fertilizers and manures, gelatine, and even high-priced cosmetics for delicate skin."[71]

Back in the city, the ragpickers, most of whom are women and children, have their special areas and deal with particular middlemen, who purchase what they collect and lend them money. They can get one rupee for a kilogram of paper or glass, a little more for cardboard, three rupees for metal, and as much as twelve rupees for plastic, depending upon the quality. They tend to specialize in one or two materials, sorting and segregating what they have collected before turning it in to a local buyer, known as *kabidi wallah*, with whom they may have been doing business for years. He weighs and buys the materials, arranges for the washing of bottles and other processing, and packs the materials into burlap bundles, which are then sold to wholesalers, who in turn sell to industrialists for recycling. His markup is said to be about 30 percent, and then the wholesaler takes another 45 percent. The kabidi wallah will often give scavengers an advance and usually some cloth to the women at festival times.

The reaction of the American author Paul Theroux was perhaps typical when his Bengali traveling companion said that all of the sidewalk dwellers were ragpickers, and consequently Calcutta's garbage was the most intensively recycled in the world: "It seemed an unusual choice of words and it strayed close to claptrap: vitality in a place where people lay dead in the gutter . . . the overdramatized quarter of a million recycling ragpickers." When the alternative is destitution, can the value of scavenging, however repugnant it may appear, be so easily dismissed? It is an organized way of life in which each patrols his or her own area and deals with a network of contacts. Understandably, scavengers say that they do not like what they have to do and hope that their children will not have to do it. But despite low status, low earnings, and low self-esteem, they regard it as their vocation, allowing them at least to eke out some sort of regular income.[72]

Working with leather, which has always been considered an inferior occupation in the Indian context, remains a niche reserved to certain minorities and castes. The oldest of the tanners are the Chinese. They settled in the Tangra area in east Calcutta, where there are about one hundred big and three hundred small tanneries. All but a few are owned by the Chinese. These tanneries usually have three floors, the ground floor being used as work space, the first floor as living quarters, and the top floor for drying leather. The raw material is supplied mostly by Muslims, while the purchaser and exporters of the finished products are mainly Punjabis. Other Chinese are bootmakers, in addition to being carpenters and cabinetmakers. Their establishments, which are located around Lower Chitpur Road in the center of the city, also combine workshops with residences.

Another group of tanners and shoemakers are Harijans, who occupy the lowest status in the Hindu social hierarchy. Mainly from Bihar, they settled in slum settlements in the Tangra-Tiljala area, where the first slaughterhouse was located. Some of them work in the Chinese tanneries as wage labor. Others own small tanning units and use mostly skin from the heads of cattle or buffaloes, rarely whole hides. They live in tiny huts and use open pits, which they lease, for processing the hides. Another small group manufactures toy drums out of the intestines of slaughtered cattle.

The Harijan bustee in Tiljala developed in the early 1920s when a wealthy person of the Chamar caste acquired the land in order to construct a number of rows of huts to rent out to his fellow caste members. Their huts are small, dark, and windowless, with an average of six persons, mainly males, sharing a single hut, even sleeping in shifts in order to accommodate as many persons as possible. Every year from May to August, they go back to their villages for the planting season, which is also a lean season for the shoe making business. They come back to Calcutta in time for the autumn festive season when new shoes are in demand. When they grow old they retire to their villages, giving way to the younger generation, which takes possession of their huts. To take fresh possession would entail paying some two thousand rupees in key money.

A common dialect binds them together in an alien urban situation and stifles potential conflicts between thika tenants and hut occupants and between owners and workers in the workshops. "The common experience of caste oppression at their place of origin, the stigma attached to their caste occupation, the continued feeling of difference from other castes in the city always remind them of their Harijan identity." As an expression of their caste solidarity, they formed a committee which solicits funds from the municipality and voluntary organizations for various welfare activities. In 1984 the committee planted a banyan tree at the entrance of the bustee.

The tree grew fast and earned a religious connotation. The Muslims in the surrounding bustees apprehended that the tree would grow further and become the centre of religious activities of the Chamars.

The tree would also spread its shade over the mosque. . . . The Muslims soon organized themselves and put pressure on the Chamars to uproot the tree, which Chamars were adamant to protect. [It was finally settled with the intervention of the political leaders] that the Chamars would encircle the tree with a brick wall and will see that it does not spread up to the mosque.[73]

"I am of low caste, I was born in vain." The lament of the untouchables has gradually been effaced by generations of labour as tanners, artisans and factory workers. . . . They have gained status which they could have never acquired in the village. They are free of the petty persecution of the village, but also removed from the urban mainstream. . . .

Yards hung with cow and buffalo carcasses, whole hides stuffed with sawdust. The hair of the dead animals lies strewn like a carpet. Here, among the tin and tiled roofs, the smoke, dust and chemicals, generations of Chamars live out their working lives. . . . Every night in this little community, the old village is brought to mind in rustic songs sung to the *dholak,* cymbals and leather *dampha.* On holiday mornings, people sit around and drink toddy. . . . The ties of blood, clan and village, cousin and kin, are strong here. So is the sway of quacks, witch-doctors and spirit-raisers. A breed of minstrel has also been brought over from the village to recite the verses of [the Harijan poet] Sant Ravi Das and sing traditional melodies. . . . On holidays too, people set out from Tangra to arrange a match for their offspring in Sodepur or Kasba, where there are settlements of their caste brethren. Or they may set aside the day to resolve a dispute over their poor property. All in all, there is a perceptible desire to hold on to the village way of life. . . .[74]

The small tanners have persistently resisted resettlement to outlying areas where pollution can be better controlled and where they can modernize their operations, organize a cooperative, and qualify for bank loans. Whatever resettlement area may be proposed, it is always too far from the rawhide wholesale market, the modern Chinese factories where many of them work, and their network of Punjabi buyers and distributors. Besides, they do not want to be separated from the ties of social neighborhood built up over the years, however congested, insanitary, and unsafe, and the investments they have made in tanning pits and sheds, however odoriferous and polluting they may be. Living as they do in a fringe area of the city, they have benefited little from bustee improvement. Although some upgrading has been done, the overall impression is bleak and cheerless: lanes thick with garbage and, during the monsoons, knee-deep in mud, latrines uncovered, and electric power not functioning. Compounding these problems of habitat is an undercurrent of communal anxiety and violence. It is not necessarily of an intercaste nature, but born of sheer frustration, an unfocused lashing out. When there is a spark, smoldering personal animosities can easily escalate into general confrontations having religious overtones.

According to press reports, Tangra is controlled by criminal elements who exploit the Chinese tannery owners. If the owners do not pay what is demanded of them for protection, they find themselves one day robbed of a hundred pieces of finished leather or other valuable property. *Mastan*—toughs or musclemen—demand from the Chinese restaurants and middle-class households in the area exorbitant amounts as puja subscriptions, while the bureaucrats and police officers who frequent the restaurants turn a blind eye. Many huts were burned down after the destruction of the mosque at Ayodhya in December 1992. The attacks were sometimes ascribed to Muslim gangs seeking revenge, other times simply to the "antisocials and miscreants." There was speculation that they had been encouraged by landlords who wanted to clear their properties to sell them for development. This is not uncommon where slums occupy valuable land adjacent to low- and middle-income housing. Resentments arising from real estate interests can easily explode and take on religious connotations. As long as the residents do not have title to land, "the sharks will circle around" (as the local press describes it) and will use thugs to terrorize the slum in order to take control of the land.

It goes without saying that the tanneries of Tangra and Tiljala in east Calcutta are not on the tourist itinerary. Tourists will hire a taxi, though, to take them to Kumartuli in the northern part of the city. This quarter is inseparably linked with the sentiments of millions of Hindu worshippers. It is where the religious images are made: the ten-armed Durga, consort of Shiva, with three eyes and black, flowing hair, who rides a lion and destroys demons; Kali, a more terrifying form of the goddess, with her black skin, bloodred protruding tongue, and garland of skulls; Ganesh, with his enormous stomach, four arms, and elephant trunk, and a rat at his feet.

Images of these and other deities in a range of sizes and forms are made from bundles of straw tightly bound into shape with protrusions of wire and bamboo. The forms are then smeared with gray clay, which is smoothed delicately along the many arms and other distinguishing features, and painted in bright colors. They are purchased just prior to the important pujas that are celebrated in the late fall and winter, the large ones by clubs for exhibit in the elaborately decorated pandals that are set up in each neighborhood, the small ones for display at home. When the celebrations have ended, the effigies are returned to the sacred river, where they are allowed to dissolve back into their original constituents—clay, straw, and bamboo.

Big landlords who once lived in this area brought in members of the Kumar caste from a neighboring district and settled them here in order to have the images made. Now other castes are involved, including refugees from East Bengal and potters from outlying districts, who come to Kumartoli before Durga Puja in October, when some six hundred potters are employed in this work. The number hired from outside exceeds the number of family workers who live in the area. For the peak season there is need for this additional skilled labor, but during the summer slack season there is much unemployment.

Image makers are strongly attached to the area where their ancestors have been working for two hundred years. Being near the Hooghly, they have the principal raw materials they need, clay and paddy straw, readily on hand. They work in one-story rented sheds, where they also live. The main constraint is lack of space. The lanes are too narrow for carts and automobiles, and there is no room to display the finished idols. During the peak work season, four or five families are jammed together in a dark and airless hutment. "With bent heads amongst crowded dolls, they exercise their artistic skills in giving shape to the dolls. . . . What they need most is space in order to stand upright and to observe their work from a distance."[75] These are the same artists whose work is exported outside of Calcutta, to Assam, Nepal, even to the United Kingdom and the United States.

They complain that the intrusion of outside producers making cheaper, lower-quality idols is hurting their business. This is inevitable as festivals become increasingly lavish and commercialized. Many years ago the festivals were fewer, simpler, more personal, and more genuine in spirit. Then the artisans of Kumartuli had a monopoly in the making of idols. The painters and potters elsewhere were mainly occupied in the manufacture of earthen toys, which are now made only in the off-season, as subsidiary work. With the greater demand for elaborate images nowadays, these artisans have turned to image making, creating new competition for Kumartuli.[76]

Not far from Kumartuli is Simlapara, where the Kansari, or brass worker caste of artisans, settled many years ago. Their densely built quarter in north central Calcutta is traversed by two or three streets clogged with vehicular traffic. The rest of their quarter is a warren of narrow lanes accessible only on foot or by rickshaw. A few small bustees, tucked away behind the multistory buildings, are occupied by Harijan Bengalis.

The Kansaris settled in the area two hundred years ago and gained a monopoly control over the production and trade in bell metal and brass water jars, pots, plates, and other household utensils. Some Hindus would never be caught eating off of anything else. Kansari also dealt in rustproof fittings for ships and related brass products. They were primarily traders (hence properly known as *kansa banik*); the actual forging and hammering was done by other castes who came from outside Calcutta and were trained by the Kasaris. After learning the skill, workers were often adopted into the community in every respect.

During the Second World War the raw material needed for their work became unavailable, and with Partition their markets in East Bengal, Burma, and beyond were cut off. At about the same time, the introduction of cheap enamel and aluminum wares and the increasing use of glass and porcelain in the Bengali households of the city closed off the local market for bell metal products. With the demise of the industry, some of the workers returned to their villages in West Bengal, and even today you can buy in the market samples of their work, sold by weight and only available in particular shops.

The Kansari have now converted to making jewelry and setting precious stones and thus continue to make their living by something akin to their traditional calling. Similarly, another group of kansa baniks who settled in Bhowanipur in south Calcutta turned gradually to gold and silversmithing. During the two world wars they saw the need for brass buttons, badges, and buckles, and, more recently, they have taken up the manufacture of parts of electrical machinery and surgical instruments. Thus, both communities have evinced their general preference for individual crafts as opposed to employment in public or commercial establishments. In Simlapara these now marginalized craftsmen, whose forebears represented a flourishing artisanal tradition, work in small workshops on a very small, made-to-order scale. As N.K. Bose pointed out, the Kansari have tried to remain as close as possible to their hereditary monopoly, with only the minimum of adaptation that was required to respond to changing demands.[77]

Kansari solidarity is reinforced by endogamy, shared traditions, and worship of their local deity, who taught them their craft. They have their neighborhood temple, although it now serves other castes in Simlapara as well. Pride in being identified as Kansari has not waned. Their temple, myths, and local divinities still have vitality. Their principal goddess who first taught them bell metal work, although no longer relevant, remains the object of a one-day festival in the autumn festival season.

Their simple two-room apartments in dilapidated buildings are typical of the genteel poor, the proud bhadralok who have fallen on hard times. The changes in their traditional calling have undermined the extended family on which their society depended. With the spread of education, particularly of girls, and more intercaste marriage, some of the younger generation have turned to other vocations or moved out of the neighborhood altogether. But a vestige of the extended family tradition lingers on: relatives occupy or lay claim to apartments in the same building.

Caste alone cannot adequately describe the poor in a city as diverse as Calcutta. Leaving aside the Muslim and Christian communities, where the equivalent of caste plays a lesser part, there are modern vocations Hindus perform which have tenuous, if any, caste antecedents of a traditional nature; for example, that of radio or auto repairman, elevator operator or receptionist, bus driver or fare collector. There is still value, even so, in isolating traditional occupations, such as leather worker, potter, or brass worker, where caste has retained some of its past relevance in facilitating urban access and adaptation. It then becomes clear that old and new migrants with different caste origins are gradually coalescing into homogeneous urban occupational units, where caste has much less importance. Caste and kinship relationships were at one time essential in providing access to livelihoods in an alien environment—even if that only meant that the most menial tasks would be available. After gaining a foothold, there were few caste restrictions to prevent the individual from improving his status and benefiting from social distinctions which still remained strong. At the same time, the continuation of traditions and attachment to caste deities and myths and places of origin provided the poor with important psychic support in dealing with urban uncertainties.

Nor does creed alone constitute an occupational barrier or determine the work that someone does. This is seen particularly in occupations which before Partition were the preserve of Muslims. The small chemical plants in the Manicktala slum in east Calcutta were once owned by Muslim Bengalis and worked mainly by Muslim migrants from Bihar. Later, many of the plants were taken over by East Bengal Hindus who moved into the area after Partition. Similarly, in Metiaburuz, a center of the tailoring and garment industry for generations, Muslim Bengalis worked in family units, the children learning the skills as apprentices. Their work was made-to-order and called for close relationships with their clientele. When the East Bengal refugees arrived, the Muslim tailors trained some of them, creating competition which would inevitably undermine their comfortable monopoly. More and more Hindus entered the business, concentrating on sewing and selling ready-made garments. The highly personalized relationships upon which the Muslims depended gave way to a thriving ready-made market in which Metiaburuz tailors sold their garments to wholesalers and retailers. One advantage Hindus had in taking over the lion's share of this market was that their women also took part in the business.

Another trade that was once exclusively in the hands of Muslims was bindery work, considered inferior by Hindus. After Partition, however, many Hindu refugees rented accommodations in the slums of the bindery quarter, known as Daftaripara. They took jobs in the hundreds of large and small firms that were engaged in book and notebook binding, envelope making, labeling, file making, numbering, punching, and sorting of scraps from heaps of paper refuse. Life stories of some of the workers tell of Hindu refugees who were grateful for the treatment they received from Muslim owners and workers. They show that continuance of a worker in the service of a particular firm was more a matter of interpersonal relations and understanding than of any specified terms of appointment.[78] Hinduism in this business posed no barrier to employment.

What makes cities like Calcutta fascinating is that it is still possible, with a little effort, to discover thriving remnants of traditional caste-based localities. Areas occupied by low-caste Hindus may still exhibit a high degree of caste solidarity, which comes from an attachment to home villages and social isolation from the mainstream bhadralok culture. In other quarters, local solidarity is expressed not only in the composition of the population, their livelihoods, social functions, and religious rites, but also in the physical layout.

> As one goes through the narrow, meandering lanes and by-lanes in the core of Bhowanipur, one recalls the days of the past in which society still preserved its old traditions. The area along the Adi Ganga is a well-integrated, old residential area which has not faced the rapid infiltration of population with diversity of interests; and the society here holds the remnants of the age-old traditional groups based on caste. . . . Though the social order has changed much due to new ways of earning and new social ideals, yet a stable parochial consciousness prevails in this neighbourhood which is lacking in the eastern section of Bhowanipur. This local solidarity is not only seen in the population composition, livelihood pattern, social functions and religious rites but is also revealed in the physical layout which has remained almost unchanged.[79]

Although caste no longer provides the bond it once did in holding families and communities together, its vestiges are still evident in neighborhood pride and, among the older generation, the retention of myths, religious ceremonies, and traditional theater. The lives of the older generation are still anchored by nostalgia for the past, whereas the yearnings of the younger generation are more directed towards the future and better expressed in mawkish soap operas, loud music, and games. Even in some slums (such as Kidderpore) which have a reputation for gambling, prostitution, and drug addiction, there is evidence of a strong and cohesive social life, of Muslims' concern for their Hindu neighbors, and Hindus' for Muslims. In this respect, Calcutta, with its bhadralok traditions of liberalism and secularism, is fortunate. Many of its neighborhoods are still associated with occupational niches, which provide security in an economy of scarcity, and thus the bonds that hold society together. What was written most cogently about an Ankara shantytown holds especially true in Calcutta: "Those peoples whose cultures can harbor extensive slum life without decomposing will be, relatively speaking, the future's winners."[80]

Providing Livelihoods

A census done in 1876 includes among the city's "lower orders" butlers, cooks, gardeners, punkah pullers, barbers, water carriers, washermen, palanquin bearers, coachmen, boatmen, porters, flower sellers, confectioners, street musicians, singers, actors, dancers, jugglers, prostitutes, potters, bangle makers, clay modelers, braziers, oil makers, salt makers, "and the first generation of the industrial proletariat—the jute and textile-mill workers. . . ."[81] About the lives of these ordinary people we know almost nothing. The accounts of old Calcutta dwelled almost exclusively on the colonial life of expatriates, with only occasional anecdotal observations regarding the activities of the native elite. Rarely do we get more than a superficial glimpse of the life of the anonymous artisan or laborer.

One story tells of a tailor who was doing very well. By the 1830s, his rich patrons had shifted their business to the new English tailoring firms, and the tailor gradually sank into poverty. His deprivation was not unique. Toward the end of the nineteenth century, the once-prosperous artisans and craftsmen had joined the ranks of the lowliest laborers. The *Report on Conditions of the Lower Classes of Bengal* observed in 1888, "as their occupations are hereditary, and are changed with difficulty, they suffer much when any alteration in trade renders their particular handicrafts unremunerative."[82]

Artisans always faced problems in obtaining the raw materials needed for their work. Trade in cotton yarn, on which weavers in the villages used to depend, was in the hands of a chain of middlemen: the dealers, mainly Marwaris, who imported the yarn from abroad; those who bought from them on wholesale; and finally the retailers. Each added his markup, which he passed on to the country weaver. For capital, the weaver had to resort to *mahajan* (moneylenders), yarn dealers, or cloth merchants, who were often one and the same person. Once indebted, it was almost impossible to escape the mahajan's clutches. In fact, from the moneylender's point of view a little indebtedness was a safeguard during the months when the weaver was likely to become a defaulter. As the dominant partner, he set the terms and conditions in his own favor, leaving only a bare subsistence to the actual worker. Now, a hundred years later, the system has little changed.

> In Garden Reach . . . some 3000 tailor families have been caught for years in a complex web, where from purchase of cloth to sale of garment several middlemen are involved. The cloth wholesaler sells to one middleman on credit (usually at a marked-up price), that middleman delivers the cloth to another with an order for garments, the second one engages a master tailor to cut the pieces, and the pre-cut pieces are delivered to tailoring families for stitching. A family of husband and wife and two children toiling almost round the clock can hardly make 150 rupees a month, for the remuneration is absurdly low. Current rates are less that three rupees for a dozen children's shirts. Buttonholes and buttons are paid for at the rate of five rupees per hundred. It is the tailoring family that has to pay for the thread and upkeep of the sewing machine. . . . It is not that the first and the second middlemen make all the money. The person who buys up the garments, the wholesaler who stocks the garments, and the retailer who finally sells them are also there, nibbling at the value added.[83]

Dependence on a particular skill, where any alteration in trade can render a certain type of production obsolete, only adds to insecurity and makes the power of the middlemen all the more intrusive:

> There is a village within the Calcutta Metropolitan District where ninety per cent of the population has been engaged for more than two generations in making brushes for shoes and cloths from animal hair backed by wood. In spite of the villagers' skill, which is admittedly high, and the experience accumulated over such a long period, they are still completely in the grip of the middlemen who control the supply and price of animal hair. Also, none in the village has diversified any further into other kinds of brushes or products. Hence, any technological advance such as the cheap production of synthetic hair brushes could ruin the whole village. Similarly, any large-scale unit which can cut out the middleman and get the animal hair cheaper will be able to undercut the entire group of villages even at the current scale of wages, low though it is.[84]

Fragmented by origin, language, and caste, the poor never organized to address common complaints and resist exploitation. Even the first industrial workers, coming from agricultural communities and displaced artisan groups, took a long time to emerge into an articulate, organized class. The unions which sprang up during the Swadeshi movement disappeared without leaving a trace. It was not that the workers were contented. In the jute mills three shifts worked day and night and were lodged in shameful conditions. A working family could not expect but a single room in which "to live, eat, sleep, propagate their species, and die," and often two families lived in one room.[85]

At the time of independence, the economy of Calcutta was dominated by jute mills, the export of gunny sacks and other jute products, and tea from the gardens upcountry around Darjeeling. Although for a while jute continued to be the largest employer of organized labor in the metropolitan area, increasing difficulties in obtaining raw jute from East Pakistan and competition from new jute mills there led to a decline in the number of workers employed. With each poor crop and with each industrial dispute, a piece of the world market for jute products was lost to synthetic substitutes. Deep recession in the late sixties, labor unrest, and shortages of raw materials as well as investment capital because of political instability contributed to industrial stagnation. Calcutta's port, once the premier port in India, steadily declined because of silting up of the Hooghly, excess capacity, and competition from other ports, especially Bombay. Since then, new industries have invariably set up their operations in other cities, and the level of industrial production in Calcutta has declined, while production on a national scale has risen.[86]

Many of Calcutta's traditional industries, notably textiles, heavy engineering, jute, paper, and rubber, became so "sick" that they had to be taken over by the government of West Bengal. Between 1973 and 1981 the government took over close to fifty large-scale industries, saving a total of 26,900 jobs. But during each year of that period many times that number of jobs were lost owing to closures, lockouts, and other industrial disputes.

Only certain light engineering, craft, and service industries showed any appreciable growth, and this occurred largely in small-scale and household enterprises. In marked contrast to the decline in traditional manufacturing and processing, the tertiary sector (trade, commerce, and finance) has been steadily increasing over the past two decades, as reflected in increased sales tax collections. Growth rates in manufacturing and processing have been consistently higher in Bombay than in Calcutta. Only with respect to very small enterprises has Calcutta shown dynamic growth in recent years.[87]

When large-scale industries have failed to meet needs, industries and services in the informal or unorganized sector have come up to fill the gap. The category "informal sector" is of course broad and imprecise. It is characterized by a mass of small-scale artisan and service activities catering to personal needs. It includes self-employed entrepreneurs and small family-owned enterprises, which employ unpaid family members, apprentices, and wage earners at subsistence wages. They rely heavily on indigenous and recycled materials, using labor-intensive methods. They offer personalized service at low cost and under flexible credit arrangements the poor can afford. They take on jobs others are unwilling to handle. Laundering, house cleaning, and other services are provided wherever household incomes are too small for the purchase of appliances but large enough to command the services of laundrymen and sweepers. Utilizing idle resources, mainly labor, the informal sector adds to the range and quantity of goods and services available to the poor and not-so-poor alike: providing quick cheap meals to the working class and even basic health services such as dental and eye care at prices the poor can afford, as well as personal services, such as housework and child care for middle-class and wealthy families. It encompasses socially useful activities like the recycling of garbage as well as the making of entirely trivial items such as homemade ink, odd medicinal recipes, cheap toys, and strings of beads. Where capital-intensive services have failed, informal sector services have met the need. When electricity is not available because of power shortages, household industries produce the candles and lanterns for which there is then a demand.

Much of this activity takes place on the sidewalks and in the slums. Tailoring, leather work, shoe making, and the manufacture of plastic buttons, combs, tubs, bottles, electrical and electronic components, and a host of other products abound in the bustees. Some of the work is subcontracted out by modern plants in the vicinity. Heat sealing of plastic bags or pressing out rubber washers and gaskets for electric fans and other appliances are examples of this. Other industries are entirely indigenous to the slums, such as the salvaging of plastic, which is collected by bustee children, cleaned, cut up, and pulverized into small bits for recycling into plastic molds in another group of bustee industries, through a process of heating and melting in electric furnaces. The informal sector also includes the plumbers, furniture makers, electricians, TV repairmen, masons, messengers, hawkers, rickshaw pullers, and carters who live in the slums, as well as the barbers, practitioners of folk medicine, musicians, artists, preparers of sweetmeats, *churi-*

har, who make glass bangles, and *mirshikar,* who trap and deal in birds. The growing affluence of traders, transporters, and others operating out of congested commercial areas puts pressure on demand for urban land for the construction of office space, apartments, and shops. Under such conditions, the informal sector flourishes. Increased construction and transport activities create earning opportunities for hawkers, petty traders, garment manufacturers, and many other services. As long as there is a large surplus of labor, these services will continue to absorb great numbers of the unskilled at low rates of compensation, while in times of economic stagnation, employment in the informal sector is all that enables such workers to scratch out a subsistence. Thus in bad times as well as good it remains the manpower market of last resort. No wonder it is regarded almost as a panacea for the unemployment endemic in Third World cities. The informal sector has become a buzzword in development circles.

There is an important caveat, however: Informal sector activity operates in intensely competitive markets. It comprises a high degree of underemployment and shared poverty: three or four persons dividing a task which could as well be done by one, market women sitting for hours in front of little piles of fruit or vegetables, barbers and shoe shiners squatting on the sidewalk all day to serve only a handful of customers, young boys dodging in and out of traffic selling tissues, wiping car windows, hawking magazines or cigarettes individually, construction workers waiting each morning, often in vain, in the hope of going out on a job.

This visibility of underemployment and redundant employment leaves the impression that the informal sector is inefficient, parasitic, and economically unproductive. But there are hidden efficiencies in the bustle of street trading and chains of middlemen who break down supplies into smaller and smaller parcels and send them on their way with minimum cost, say, in warehousing and transportation. Because the informal sector provides livelihoods and supplementary income to many people, as well as goods and services to a mass, low-income market, and so many people are thus surviving, even happily, it cannot be regarded as unproductive or marginal.

Still, the jobs that are created are precarious and barely pay a living wage. Work is often irregular. The worker is isolated, without bargaining power or any kind of insurance against old age, sickness, or accident. Often female and child labor are preferred because they are cheaper. Nirmala Banerjee of the Center for Studies in Social Sciences in Calcutta concludes that families where all members work in the informal sector must send out at least three earners to ensure an income above the poverty level because wage rates are significantly lower than what is paid for comparable work in the formal sector:

> The officially-fixed minimum wage for *biri* rolling in workshops is now Rs. 3.50 to Rs. 4.25 per thousand *biris* when the worker is given both the tobacco and the leaves to roll them in. . . . Women who take the same work home get only Rs. 1.50 to Rs. 2.50 per thousand *biris*. Similarly, the technique of assembling radios is the same whether done on factory premises or farmed out to small workshops, but the average wage rate in the latter is about one-fourth that of the former.[88]

Slum entrepreneurs operate in a singularly unfavorable business environment. The absence of bank financing necessitates borrowing against orders of consignment or from moneylenders at three times the rate charged by banks. Work in the bustees takes place in a claustrophobic cubicle or in the corner of a room with no convenient access to customers. Inputs are obtained on the open market, or the black market, in small quantities and at higher prices than would be paid by large producers, who can get raw materials through manufacturers or through the government at controlled rates. Profit margins are miniscule because of middlemen and markups. There are also other costs in doing business: a bribe to the store to ensure that the goods will not be rejected, to the purchasing officer for securing the order, to the accounts officer to ensure payment without much delay, to the meter reader for the illegal electricity connection. Petty entrepreneurs are dependent upon a commercial oligarchy which profits from the cheapness of their products and the pitiful earnings of their workers but provides a real service in distributing and marketing their production. They know full well how they are cheated in the manner of price, "but it is only this exploitation that can guarantee them a means of livelihood, however meager it may be."[89]

The small bindery units in Daftaripara, typical of the informal sector, are in frantic competition for work and therefore obliged to accept orders at very low rates. Their workers are paid on a daily or piecework basis. The owners are usually also workers themselves, sharing in the uncertainties of the business. Unable to offer higher wages, because low rates and low wages are interlocked, they render petty services to hired workers, such as bringing tea or sharing cigarettes.

Location is critical in maintaining a network of personalized relationships with customers, distributors, suppliers, and moneylenders built up over time. Some enterprises may operate from shifting locations, but only within a certain prescribed area. The small metalworking establishments crowded along Belillious Road in Howra (or the image makers of Kumartuli) illustrate the importance of location, however unsatisfactory it might be in purely physical terms. These workshops produce valves, pipe fittings, bolts and nuts, hand tools, and railway components, while the general-purpose jobbing machine shops provide welding, galvanizing, and the like. They are built up wall to wall in an area that is crowded and unsanitary. To operate more than one shift is difficult because the workshops are also used as residences. Their machinery is antiquated; they function too close to the edge of subsistence to afford new machinery. There is too much uncertainty about future marketing possibilities to risk taking loans for expansion. To improve the crowded and unhealthy industrial area would require convincing some of these workshops to move out to a new industrial estate a few miles away. But this means incurring the costs for moving rickety but still serviceable equipment and the risks involved in abandoning immediate access to a network of commercial and subcontracting relationships.[90]

There is always a heavy price to pay, not only in the savagely exploitative, subhuman conditions of work that the informal sector may entail, but also in terms of loss of traditions and skills. Quoting Nirmala Banerjee again:

> Calcutta had a fine tradition for its command over many sophisticated and delicate skills. The best hand-made shoes were to be got here. The life of almost any machine could be extended till infinity because spare parts, however sophisticated, could be reproduced. The quality of delicacies in food . . . was unbelievable. The craftsmanship in gold, embroidery or tailoring was of a very high order. Now, because no craft can earn an adequate living in the city, the craftsmen are either moving out or not being replaced. Calcutta's Chinese, who were expert carpenters, shoe-makers, and cooks, have moved away. Experts in European cooking are long gone and Calcutta is rapidly losing its reputation for light engineering to other parts of the country. Now Calcutta only produces either the standardized brand names or tacky goods whose main qualification is that they are cheap.[91]

There is also a price to pay in the longer-term deterioration of human capital. Among the poor, children often have to start work as early as at the age of eight and so are unable to complete their primary education. This means that the entire blue-collar labor force will continue to be functionally illiterate for another generation. The only training that takes place is by rote learning.

> Even skilled artisans like masons or carpenters learn their jobs only by imitation. Without some basic education in subjects like geometry, mensuration, or mechanics, they have no way of adapting their knowledge to a changing market. . . . An experienced worker may be very skilled at a particular task or at the use of a tool such as a lathe; but he has no proper conception of the total potential of the tool or of the skill because he knows nothing of the basic principles behind it. Therefore, with all his ingenuity and desperation, he is usually totally dependent on others for designing his work and a change in the pattern of orders can make him totally redundant. . . .[92]

With a long tradition of serving the poor, private charitable societies have devoted their main attention to giving relief to the sick and the destitute and to running schools and clinics. With regard to economic conditions in impoverished neighborhoods, they could only scratch the surface, for example, by producing handicrafts and embroidered stoles for foreign visitors. This situation has changed in recent years as more creative approaches have been tried in an effort to create jobs.

In the early seventies, the Calcutta Metropolitan Development Authority (CMDA) and the Ford Foundation proposed a community-based program in certain bustees where physical improvements had already begun. An "apex" institution, the Calcutta Bustee Progress Association (known as KBPS, from its Bengali name) was set up with much fanfare to coordinate the work of religious and secular social welfare agencies already active in the bustees. Young community leaders were chosen in certain pilot areas to conduct surveys, meet with residents to discuss a package of social and economic activities, and draw up "integrated development plans." Emphasis was given to setting up cooperatives for making soap, glassware, safety matches, footwear, or other items for local consumption; or else cooperatives for purchasing groceries, medicines, and ready-made garments to be sold through community shops; or for providing services such as automobile, radio, and TV repair or food catering.

The initial response was positive. Families showed their eagerness to join the cooperatives. But before long opposition from various quarters began to mount. KBPS was criticized for using outside consultants and recruiting "bustee leaders" who were not the legitimate representatives of their communities. With the death of the KBPS president, who had been seen from abroad as the "hope of Calcutta," the program degenerated amid squabbles among personalities, voluntary agencies, and political factions, and the plans that had been prepared remained on the shelf. Ultimately, the program was opposed by the state government even on a pilot basis, there having been little success with cooperatives in the past. In addition there were rumblings of innuendo regarding some shady involvement on the part of the CIA—the bugbear often believed to be lurking behind any initiative that receives foreign endorsement.

An offshoot of the program known as the Small-Scale Enterprise Program managed to keep going with World Bank funding after the demise of KBPS. Special workshop areas were provided for self-employed or potentially self-employed artisans and traders in different localities: tailors in one slum, clay modelers in another, veneer makers in another, leather tanners in another. A credit scheme at concessional rates of interest was set up in cooperation with some commercial banks. Beginning slowly because of cumbersome appraisal and disbursement procedures, the credit program was later streamlined to the point where a team of bank officers would move into a bustee on an advertised date, interview borrowers, and appraise their projects, and quite often the approved borrower would walk out of the meeting with the money in his pocket.

The results were initially encouraging. Borrower incomes increased, new jobs were created, and the incidence of arrears was low. The program was expanded to include additional banks. Greatest success was achieved among tailors, which could be explained in large part by the low capital cost of adding a job: essentially the cost of a sewing machine. Also, Calcutta had emerged by that time as a major supply center for ladies' garments. But then, after a while, the repayment picture began to deteriorate. Sponsoring of borrowers became politicized. Ward councillors, as the local political leaders, had greater say in who got a loan, and decisions were made largely on political grounds. With mounting arrears, banks were reluctant to make new loans, and overall activity diminished. The sole exception was in a borough where an association of hawkers and shop owners played an active part in sponsoring borrowers. With the blessing of the dominant political party, it supplanted the ward councillors in determining who qualified for loans.

Although making credit easily available increased the income of self-employed persons, nothing was being done to reach out to those who needed skill training in order to become eligible for credit and gainfully employed. So a new program of national scope (known as Nehru Rojgar Yojana, or Nehru Income Mobilization) was introduced to provide short-term training and loans for unemployed youth. Training became available for wage employment, which would not require a loan, or for self-employment, which would. Local institutes contracted to provide training in tailoring, armature wiring, wool knitting, leather bag making, TV repair, floral art, silk screen painting, beautician skills, and yoga therapy. Families below certain income levels were eligible for loans, with "scheduled" (low-status) castes and women receiving preferential treatment. Because approval again rested with the ward councillor or alderman, whatever formula was adopted, political considerations would inevitably come into play.

The fact of the matter is that there are not many persons who, even with training and loans, can establish their own businesses in already intensely competitive markets. Job creation is an ill-defined and elusive goal under any circumstances. It can occur to a limited extent at the level of the metropolitan economy or, better yet, at the regional level, where improvements in agriculture or irrigation create demand for tools and supplies which can be produced in the city, thus stimulating employment. But within the narrow context of slum neighborhoods, where there is already a high level of underemployment and shared poverty, targeted efforts to create jobs as tried in Calcutta seem to be doomed from the start.

These initiatives are grounded on the premise that the informal sector offers a palliative, if not a solution, to the intractable problems of unemployment. Not the least of the difficulties then encountered is how to work on the smallest scale: how to reach out with appropriate services to a multitude of exceedingly small artisanal and service enterprises, each with its special requirements. Programs must be tailored to the specific conditions in each community, and each slum has unique occupational characteristics. Besides this need for precise "targeting" of assistance, there are few institutions securely rooted in the slums and enjoying the confidence of slum dwellers that are sophisticated enough to serve as a channel for outside assistance. (Examples would be cooperatives and credit unions which could link small enterprises together and furnish the credit, procurement, and marketing facilities traditionally supplied by middlemen.) Even if the inherent problems of scale and delivery could be resolved, the overall scope and opportunity for providing useful assistance would ultimately be quite limited. The majority of the slum labor force is engaged as laborers, clerks and shopkeepers, hawkers and petty traders, domestic servants and sweepers, besides those in marginal occupations such as scavenging and begging. There is little room within these vocations for any useful intervention, if not because of unwillingness to change lifestyle then because there is no perceived need for technical or other outside assistance. Among the minority engaged in small-scale and cottage industry, there is likewise little scope to improve skills or change traditional crafts which survive in spite of technological innovations.

When all is said and done, any intervention which tends to strengthen the competitiveness of some enterprises by increasing productivity through training, credit, and marketing assistance inevitably drives less efficient producers out of business. Once credit is made more easily available, the enterprises that benefit most end up becoming more capital-intensive, thus displacing labor. The support of a few means the demise of many others, thereby undermining the main redeeming feature of the informal sector, namely its capacity to absorb labor and remain the employer of last resort.

Mobilizing the Community

The neighborhood, known as a *para,* embraces several streets and lanes. It is where there is a substantial ethnic or linguistic homogeneity, an area of frequent interaction: in the tea stalls, in *adda,* or gossip groups (a quintessential Bengali institution devoted to relaxed conversation), in sports, and through the neighborhood clubs which organize social welfare and cultural activities.

There are said to be two thousand voluntary associations in Calcutta. But there must be more when all the bustee committees and neighborhood clubs are counted, some of which function only sporadically. To organize an ever-growing anonymous population and its diverse activities, the city gives rise to a plethora of these associations. Loss of kinship and village identity and the impersonality of urban relationships lead to the formation of groups which have educational, recreational, welfare, religious, and economic purposes. Some, like the Rotary, are importations, relics of colonialism and the process of westernization. Others, more numerous, are traditional and indigenous in character, such as caste organizations and mutual benefit societies. They tend to be localized whereas western offshoots are citywide.

Every slum has its youth club, which organizes sports and cultural activities even under the most crowded conditions. Lack of space does not inhibit the vitality of interaction. An alley serves well enough as a cricket pitch without serious obstruction to the flow of pedestrian traffic, a cul-de-sac as a stage for a theatrical presentation. Within the tiny, two-room clubhouse, space is reserved for carrom (a spirited type of billiards), weight lifting, a library with some Bengali, English, and Urdu books, a dusty assortment of musical instruments to be pulled out for celebrations, a TV set in seemingly constant use as young viewers follow a soap opera or episode from the great Indian epic Ramayana. Room is even made available for occasional family planning, prenatal clinics, and adult literacy classes. Members organize musical and dramatic presentations and collect subscriptions for religious festivals. Private families and caste associations used to do this, but now it is typically the younger generation that collects money for images and the elaborate pandals in its enthusiasm to outdo those put up in other neighborhoods. One club purchased a satellite dish and sells cable services to families in the area. When garbage is not collected, young men go to the authorities to complain, and when flooding occurs they might even rebuild the drains themselves. They also act as vigilantes to protect the community against the thugs who are said to infest the area.

These community activists may be well into their twenties or in their early thirties. There are no exclusively female clubs, at least in the Muslim bustees. Clubs are patronized by prominent, older members of the community, one of whom may be the president in an honorific capacity. Some clubs have been around for a long time. A physical culture club founded in 1900 still runs weight lifting competitions and does social welfare work, such as providing voluntary nursing in times of sickness and assisting destitute members of the community in meeting the expense of cremation.

Calcutta in the late 1960s was out of control. Faced with political unrest and worsening decay, the government had to move quickly. A 1.5-billion-rupee development program had been prepared which would put 100,000 persons to work laying the first sewers in areas containing more than half of the metropolitan population, cleaning accumulated silt out of the water treatment plant and building pretreatment facilities, renovating streetcars, and improving the bustees. Emphasis was placed on upgrading infrastructure, on engineering solutions, with CMDA having overall authority and serving as the coordinating body. Because of the indifferent performance of weak functional agencies, CMDA extended its authority and soon emerged as "a gigantic public works construction empire." CMDA's logo appeared everywhere as streets were excavated, roads widened, drainage ditches dug, and bustees fitted out with latrines, standpipes, paving, and lighting. The Authority's engineers talked of integrating the bustee sewerage systems with that of the metropolitan area. But what bustee dwellers would experience, at least where sewer lines had not been installed, were blocked toilets because septic tanks could not handle the additional discharge. As an evaluation of the program by the World Bank concluded, the mind-set of the engineer was inappropriate in dealing with poverty. The goals were never that clear-cut, and there were no purely technical answers.[93]

The bustees had been largely cut off from the rest of the city, shunned by other citizens, and ignored for decades by government officials. Ethnically separate, they were a world apart, with their own markets and moneylenders. Bonds of common origin and culture were strong. After a history of property seizure and forcible eviction, they had every reason to view with suspicion any show of outsider interest and concern. Any investigation into conditions was seen by residents as threatening, and met with resentment. The people remained disease-ridden and uneducated. They were living only to survive, their leisure spent playing cards or squatting by the roadside. They had no community centers, schools, health clinics, or facilities for sports and games.

Bustee needs obviously went well beyond engineering solutions. To attend to these needs, CMDA had to depend on other government departments and the complementary programs of social service agencies. It recruited a small core of social workers to establish the initial contact with the bustee people and secure their cooperation in carrying out physical improvements and in setting up clinics and schools. A few nutrition centers were established, "small islands of hope" in the words of someone involved at the time. Some space had been found or some money collected locally to build the center, which later could be expanded to include a primary class or craft training. Masons, carpenters, and other skilled workers living in the bustees lent a hand. Young men and women worked, without remuneration, as primary school teachers, medical assistants, and in adult literacy centers. Gradually the government brought these self-help initiatives under its wing, paying teachers and including children in its feeding programs.

Bustee youth clubs and neighborhood associations helped in locating sanitary latrines and water taps and dealing with illiterate families. Slum dwellers did not believe at first that anyone was willing to help them without imposing some sort of financial burden. Ordinarily their only contact with politicians and government engineers was when they came around at election time to inspect the drains, express appropriate concern—and do nothing. And that was the last slum residents saw of them for another few years. There had to be some ulterior motive. But suspicions soon abated and enthusiasm built up, as described by Sudhendu Mukherjee, the CMDA sociologist on the scene:

> It is a forgotten chapter of history now how these bustee youths stood by the side of the engineers, contractors and construction labourers . . . day in and day out under blazing sun, in torrential rains and cold wintery nights . . . pointing out the most convenient location for latrines, water taps, and street lights.[94]

Big changes were taking place. A school, initially set up under a tent and staffed by volunteer teachers, eventually evolved into a six-room building where preprimary classes, two primary shifts (Bengali and Urdu), and literacy and embroidery classes for adults were given, in addition to serving as a UNICEF distribution center and dispensary. Available space was utilized for a variety of purposes, even if it meant holding two classes back-to-back in the same room, one class facing the teacher at one end of the room, another facing the opposite direction, while just outside, a cacophony of horns, shouts, and general hubbub.

Bhadralok traditions of liberalism and humanism, tempered with the spirit of noblesse oblige, have always found expression through charitable organizations that did things for the poor. This benevolent legacy dates back to the last century, when venerable families living in the vicinity of a bustee donated land or money for a school or social center and handed out food and cloth to the destitute on religious holidays. Societies were formed to help lepers, paupers, beggars, and refugees from famine and flood, to assist needy students with free books and tuition, and to organize health education by conducting calisthenics. Orphanages and rescue homes were founded in the wake of the ceaseless flow of refugees. During the 1950s, communist activists organized bustee residents to resist eviction. Some of the committees which were formed at that time remained moderately active, engaged perhaps in programs to drive out antisocials and protect the morals of bustee girls. Later, with the support of welfare societies, they set up sewing centers and distributed milk and bread to the children.

The multipurpose nature of welfare societies emerged during the turbulent early years of this century, when political associations were banned, and social and cultural centers served as a subterfuge for political agitation. Today, welfare societies run schools with volunteer teachers, literacy classes, homeopathic clinics, and craft training. Retired civil servants and professionals do volunteer service in the bustees. Some of them run schools that serve special categories of pupils, such as the children of prostitutes and of particular artisan castes. The wives of railway officials set up a school for the children who live on the platforms of the two main railroad stations. Günter Grass dedicated his book

Show Your Tongue to an elderly couple ("they come from Brahman families, but that was long ago forgotten, like childhood diseases") who have for many years run a school for the garbage and slum children in the Dhapa dump area.

The United Bustee Development Association (UBDA), which works in the predominantly Muslim bustees and adjacent squatter settlements of Tijala and Beniapukur, is representative of this humanist tradition. Finding the area a "noisy, quarreling place of antisocials," it surveyed the families and prepared proposals which it submitted to nongovernmental organizations (NGOs) for funding. It called together the people for a workday to build the foundation of a community center. The next year, the ground floor was completed and classes begun, days for primary and evenings for nonformal instruction, volunteer teachers getting the equivalent of ten dollars a month. With material support from UNICEF, children were vaccinated and mothers were given family planning advice. The bustee youth club won the football tournament in 1985, attracting attention well beyond the confines of the community. UBDA approached banks for loans to help working women earn additional income from tailoring, paper bag making, and toy making, and marriage aid was given to a number of families "to help them get rid of dowry taking."

Since bustee improvements began in the early seventies, there has been no letup in the formation of local committees representing the residents. The proliferation of new committees and groups can be attributed to the erosion of ethnic exclusiveness and the emergence of a more impersonal urban culture, a melting pot of sorts. But some groups are obviously parasitic. Where once was a single bustee committee, now there are several, all officially registered and competing for funds. Some are linked to politicians who seek to refurbish their image by being identified with grass-roots interests, others to bureaucrats who hold slum constituencies in their pockets to bring out when funds are about to be allocated. A committee, once inactive except for a few days during the festival season, now claims to run a full-time health care and education program which, it argues, deserves sustained financial support. Personal and special interests take precedence over the interests of the community at large.

The spawning of new groups, all scrambling to get onto the NGO bandwagon, also gives rise to more elaborate structures and need for greater coordination. Working in three Kidderpore wards that once had a reputation as hotbeds of crime and antisocial activity, the Bastibasi Samannaya Samity (Bustee Dwellers Co-ordination Committee) acts as an intermediary between youth clubs, individual bustee committees, NGO sources of funding, and the municipal authorities. Its executive committee includes representatives of twenty Hindu and Muslim bustee committees (its vice president being a woman from one of the Muslim bus-tees). When different ethnic groups live in one bustee there will be two or three committees in which youth clubs are represented. This grass-roots structure has been effective in bridging the com-munal gap: Muslim-Hindu peace prevailed after the Ayodhya incident at a time when other areas were being rocked by riots.

Stemming from the early tradition of benevolence and the innate proclivities of the NGOs, emphasis was invariably placed on providing sustenance to the unfortunate. Little attention was given to developing indigenous capabilities. Even though this distinction between welfare and development becomes somewhat murky under poverty conditions, CMDA and the World Bank stressed the need to break out of the conventional "welfare men-tality" which had hitherto characterized NGO involvement.

The Calcutta Urban Services Consortium (CUSCON) was set up to coordinate the activities of some two dozen social welfare agencies and to incorporate development-oriented approaches into their slum programs. This it did reasonably well until it became beneficiary to a generous grant from the West German Protestant churches, enabling it to embark on its own indepen-dent program. Going its separate way, it was succeeded in its "apex" role by another creation, the Kalikata Bustee Pragati Sangstha (KBPS) cited above. KBPS had ten constituent NGO members, to which were added a consortium of others backed by churches in Europe. After a brief surge of optimism, impetus began to wane, and eventually all semblance of cooperation dissolved amid conflicts among agencies and personalities.

KBPS liked to think of itself as introducing programming competence and financial discipline. As an apex organization, however, it was removed from operational details and bustee-level realities. Impatient with the slow process of involving bustee representatives in neighborhood-sponsored programs, it trained its own social workers, thereby undercutting efforts to implant its activities within the community. Meanwhile, competition among participating NGOs was exacerbated by too much money from abroad. NGOs were jealous of their particular projects and their separate sources of funding. Their disposition and operating style were such that they resented efforts at central control and resisted accountability to any higher authority. Coordination meant to them infringement of their independence. Intolerant of bureaucratic requirements, which they regarded as unnecessary and petty, and the delays involved in mounting a comprehensive program along KBPS lines, they pressed ahead with short-term ameliorative activities: distributing medicines and milk, immunizing children, and dealing with individual cases of distress. The welfare mentality was too ingrained to be subordinated to what was regarded as abstract development objectives. Straightforward welfare provided more immediate gratification, and they liked to take around visitors and show them all that they were doing to help "their poor."

Quite predictably, politics deeply permeated these programs. Neighborhood clubs, once under the patronage of wealthy bhadralok families, came under the influence of particular political parties. Community-based institutions which had emerged originally from innate feelings of local solidarity were supplanted by new associations which included a wider area and had politicians on their management committees. NGOs also had their political ties. Politicians needed access through NGO social workers and community links to garner the votes of the bustee population. A political party would establish a bustee committee, turning young educated men and women into political activists. Because such groups depended upon political patronage, they were not always acceptable partners in development work, and other groups would be vitalized by particular NGOs with their ready access to international funds. Youth clubs were used to recruit field-workers or provide a room in which to have meetings, receiving in return sports equipment and other supplies. A primary school was denied government recognition because the school management committee was not in the good graces of the political leadership.

Because of KBPS's close ties with the Marxist government of West Bengal, West German funding support was eventually withdrawn. Fragmentation of NGO activities (including the split-up of CUSCON) was accompanied by a fragmentation of neighborhoods, leaving bustee residents confused in the wake of competing interests that had nothing to do with their immediate concerns. They did not understand the politics of welfare, the distinctions between acronyms, and the nuances of different agendas, priorities, and development strategies.

NGOs, moreover, are inherently conservative. They are staffed by retired civil servants and businessmen at the top and, lower down, by social workers from among the educated unemployed and by housewives and others without roots in the slums. The bustee population depends on them for assistance, while they, in turn, impose their middle-class values. Volunteer housewives, quite reasonably, might look upon improved sanitation as the highest priority; social workers might insist that education is the critical entry point from which to reach other aspects of impoverished lives. For the slum dwellers most directly concerned, however, some kind of job might be regarded as being most crucial: they can take water from the roadside tap and, if sick, can lie down and wait for recovery; in the meantime, their children must go out to work rather than attend school. Because priorities differ, there is a built-in tension between NGOs and community-based groups. To bridge the gap, one NGO employs social workers from the poor who work closely with local residents, but their effectiveness lasts only as long as they are not put on the payroll.

Arguing along these lines, some people who have worked extensively in the slums believe that Calcutta has attracted too much attention and money from abroad. In the early days of bustee improvement the Marxist government looked askance at the international NGOs and their capitalist sponsors abroad. There were consequently only a few local NGOs working with community groups. Their programs were modest and the scale appropriate, given the limited self-help capabilities of the poor communities with which they were dealing. Later, government attitudes and policies changed. Licenses were issued so that more NGOs could tap into outside sources of funds. The ensuing flood of money from governments and churches abroad swept aside whatever reserve of self-help and volunteerism may have existed. Community groups began to look outside of their own capacity. Every embassy set up its own "NGO unit," showing particular interest in big proposals which would have impact—and which, incidentally, involved amounts of money that would swamp any realistic level of community participation. From the standpoint of the foreign donor, programs had to be quick-acting and must produce tangible results in order to satisfy aid officials and legislatures back home. In their impatience, they lost sight of the value of small projects nurtured over time that could be managed by the people themselves. The bustees improved physically, but socially and politically they became polarized and more divided than ever, largely because of this competition for outside resources.

There is a familiar ring to all this. It encapsulates the sad experience of so much well-intentioned foreign aid. Amid all the apparent achievements of "development" (a word that begs many questions) lies the rubble of modest efforts on the part of ordinary people to help themselves, efforts effectively subverted by the fixation of technocrats on tidy or comprehensive solutions and the impatience of bureaucrats to commit funds and show quick results.

On the other hand, isolated, small-scale interventions by NGOs to assist a few hundred people in one bustee or another are usually not sustainable over the long run. The likelihood of any synergism with other poverty initiatives is remote, and should funds run out, well-meaning activities will most likely grind to a halt.

The health program set up under a World Bank loan is a good example of the scale that is required. The program provides basic health and family planning services to a total bustee population of 1.4 million. Relying on a highly decentralized approach, it has achieved positive results. Immunization rates have averaged over sixty percent for the major diseases and effective contraceptive rates forty percent, which are impressive figures for a population with little previous access to these services. A significant reduction in infant and maternal mortality and in crude birth rates are indications of the program's impact.[95]

The program spells out valuable lessons. It is staffed by women recruited from the areas in which they are assigned. Known as "honorary health workers," they provide services at the doorsteps of the community. This has been essential in breaking down initial suspicion among clients, many of whom assumed that the house visits were being made to gain their vote for a political party. The health workers have divided their areas into manageable blocks, and by carrying out home visits six days a week, are able to get back to each family every two weeks. Using the premises of a neighborhood association or youth club, they give their attention to pre- and postnatal care, first aid, family planning, and environmental sanitation, referring malnutrition and more complicated cases to a doctor or professional material and child health (MCH) services. This focus on a limited number of tasks is one of the strong points of the program.

Another reason for success has been the caliber and commitment of the health workers. Although receiving only a small honorarium and employed only part-time, they take obvious pride in what they are doing and in showing visitors around "their families." It was originally expected that they would be between thirty and forty-five years old and married, but it has turned out that most of them are in their twenties and unmarried.

Health work is one of the few types of professional employment available to them. They have a higher level of education than older women and fewer household and child-rearing responsibilities because they are unmarried. Indeed, being often the only income earners in their families, the poverty trap prevents them from being free to marry.[96]

Once it was the bustees that were isolated from the mainstream. Now it is the squatter settlements on sidewalks and along railway embankments and canals, which can be thought of as second-generation bustees. In some of them, Unnayan (mentioned earlier) installs wells, builds kutcha schools of bamboo, donates food and plastic sheeting when a settlement is wiped out by violence or storms, organizes women's poultry and piggery projects, and intervenes in cases of police harassment. Prantik Jana Vikas Kendra (Society for the Uplift of the Marginal People), another local organization set up originally by Unnayan and later supported by the Lutherans, runs squatter schools for children in the northeastern wards of the city. Because squatting is officially illegal, these schools are not recognized and receive no government support. Pupils are given "nonformal" instruction, which is, by and large, a poor substitute for a basic formal program. Yet the success of these schools has been more in organizing community life than in the education of the children. Many of the pupils drop out in order to work, and they could not afford the school fees even if they were qualified to go on to higher education.

Not untypical is the story of Amal who excelled in one of these sidewalk schools and planned to go on to a government school. His father was hit by a car, and the family had to sell their utensils and other belongings to buy medicine. Some middle-class neighbors also pitched in. Amal had no choice but to drop out of school. His father eventually died, and members of the squatter colony raised money for a proper *shradh* or funeral rite. But Amal could not afford to go back to school. He is now selling flowers on the roadside. He politely greets his former teacher when she regularly passes by: *didi, bhalo achhen* (dear elder sister, are you all right?).[97]

A visitor cannot help but be impressed by the sincerity of these NGO interventions. But however well intentioned, are they effectively addressing the critical environmental, security, and human rights issues? If they remain marginal, it is because of the lack of any public commitment to deal with the needs of squatters in any fundamental way. "Pay-and-use" toilets (probably installed more in deference to middle-class sensibilities than for the convenience of sidewalk dwellers) epitomize the shameful neglect of what are surely the most egregious manifestations of poverty in Calcutta. In the absence of any political will to deal with the underlying problems, sporadic and dispersed efforts on the part of NGOs can have but limited effect.

The burning issue of the day changes, it seems, with each shift in the priorities of donor governments and international agencies. AIDS is the current hot topic. HIV infection is spreading all over India; there are estimates that as many as three million people may now carry the virus. The disease epicenter is in Bombay, where an economic boom has attracted prostitutes, many of them adolescents, from Nepal and other countries. In all of West Bengal the number of HIV-positive cases is reported to be (an unbelievably low) three to four hundred, principally among prostitutes, truck drivers and their helpers, and students. The number of infected, though, will undoubtedly increase rapidly. Rickshaw pullers and children living in railway stations and bus terminals are especially at risk, and twenty NGOs have organized AIDS-awareness campaigns among their clientele in these categories.

In Calcutta as elsewhere, street children began to attract the collective attention of the international community a few years ago. Their plight became the donor preoccupation and raised prospects of generous funding. Attention focused on the tens of thousands of juveniles born in poverty and working for a pittance, collecting scrap, shining shoes, putting in long hours in tea stalls and cheap restaurants, loading vans and rickshaws, fetching and carrying, making packages and boxes in narrow rooms (where small children can move about more easily than adult workers). Of special concern were those obliged to do unhealthy and hazardous work such as breaking open dry-cell batteries in the street to reclaim the interior carbon rod, lead base, and stainless steel rings, or boiling and pouring tallow obtained from slaughterhouses for making soap, or handling decomposed materials in the dumping grounds, where there is constant danger from a sudden cave-in.

Some 75,000 to 100,000 children make their home on the streets of Calcutta. A small minority are abandoned, usually the victims of domestic quarrels, but most of them live with one or two parents. Relationships are said to be strong and loving even though children are often exploited. Dependent upon their earnings, parents have pushed them out to beg. Many youngsters find work through relatives and friends, as adults do. Laws pertaining to child labor and apprenticeship training are rarely enforced. Children usually get food and lodging, a small amount for laundering, some tips, but no assurance of regular employment. In some situations, they are in regular contact with criminals, where they get caught up in smuggling. They amuse themselves by playing cards, rolling marbles for a few paise, flying kites, and smoking cigarettes from the age of seven or eight.

They use street corners and open spaces for their toilet and take baths at public taps and hydrants. Their priority needs are food, clothing, and shelter, in that order. The worst time of year is during the monsoon, when they must stand for hours knee-deep in water with their pitiful belongings in hand. They are not attached to the city, which is alien to them. They are not tolerated by the more fortunate citizens, who regard them as urchins and thieves. They find people to be unkind compared to what they might remember from the countryside. They regard police and authority as in general hostile to them.

Their psychological needs include security and protection, recognition and praise, contentment and social acceptance. Here, girls suffer the most. Spending the whole day before the eyes of the passers-by without proper food and clothing, girls experience a strong sense of inferiority, anger, and distrust. They need to be protected from pimps, and the work they can do (there is little besides ragpicking) is more limited than in the case of boys.

UNICEF proposed a multifaceted program, which ranged from preventive health care, nutrition, and education to vocational training and legal protection against abuse and exploitation. It was administered through a system of grants to NGOs, each capable of reaching a few hundred children, and coordinated by a city-level task force including the government and the participating NGOs. But this effort, like so many others in the past, to undertake a coordinated program soon began to show signs of breaking down, in this case over salary scales, release of funds, and other bureaucratic impositions on NGOs jealous of their independence and programming flexibility.

CINI (Child in Need Institute), a local social service agency, conducted a survey of children living on the platform at Sealdah station and found their chief concerns to be somewhat different. They worried not about food, clothes, or shelter; their biggest worry was about harassment by the police. If exploited by an adult, the child's word would never be believed because the adult would claim to be the father or a relative. After that, they worried about getting sick, for hospitals would not accept the homeless. Their third concern was having a safe place to keep their money.

Exploited by drug pushers and thieves operating in the vicinity of the station, children are used as couriers, hustlers, and pimps. Little girls of ten or less have/been raped, and they have nowhere to turn; their only protection is the razor blade they conceal under their tongues, which they are able whip out in a flash. Some of them get up before dawn to pilfer vegetables, fish, and fruit when the trucks arrive at the nearby wholesale market. What they get in this way is set up in little piles and sold at prices below those of regular vendors. There is a woman on the platform whose main function it is to collect leftover rice from restaurants in the neighborhood. Rice together with some seasoning provides the children with their first meal "at 9 A.M. on platform 10 of the South Suburban line." Like adults on the verge of destitution, children also do their utmost for a semblance of an orderly existence.

CINI set up a halfway house in the station which is used for counseling, literacy training, immunizations, and, most important, a place which the children can call their own. Also, a room was donated in nearby Bowbazar as a night shelter for boys aged six to fourteen years, and another for girls, where they can cook meals for themselves. For girls living under the constant threat of sexual abuse, this shelter has special importance. The police have agreed to provide the children with identity cards, and they have been issued passbooks for recording their savings, in some cases as much as 500 rupees, or about $15, which for them is a considerable sum.

There are numerous such examples of innovative approaches, the nonformal schools run by IPER (Institute of Psychological and Educational Research) to mention another. Scavenging is done in the mornings, before the municipal trucks make their rounds, and again in the evenings, when some more refuse has accumulated. So IPER's nonformal classes, which are held on platforms, porches, and in decrepit buildings, are scheduled in the afternoon, when the children are not working. A most adverse learning environment to say the least, because of the constant din of passing traffic and trains, yet these schools have certain advantages over the public system. Children are from the immediate neighborhood and know each other. They can take their younger siblings, for whom they are responsible, to school with them. And they do not have to put up with the ridicule often showered on them in public schools by other children because of their dirty and ragged appearance.

Because children from the bustees work more regular daytime hours, IPER's classes for them are held on weekends, when the public schools are vacant. Bustee kids have their own particular needs. Generally, they take pride in having regular paying jobs in markets, tea stalls, and workshops. They can buy things. They come to school neatly attired. They would scarcely deign to sit in the same class with kids from the sidewalks and squatter colonies, who are dressed in tatters. Among slum children, too, there is a pecking order which must be observed.

Although the slums abound with these pilot activities, their combined scope remains limited, covering only a relatively small part of overall needs. Expanding discrete interventions which are successful in order to achieve a wider impact has proven to be difficult. To be absorbed within a more comprehensive program entails sacrificing the very qualities which make these private initiatives effective: the personal dedication of social workers and volunteer teachers and the flexibility to experiment as conditions dictate. To take advantage of outside resources entails accepting norms imposed from a distance, uniform procedures which inhibit innovation, progress reports, funding justifications, and other requirements which are cumbersome and time-consuming, as well as the upsetting delays in the release of funds which hamper informal, face-to-face understandings and customary ways of doing business. Because working on the small scale is imperative, much lip service is paid to decentralization, but you have to look long and hard to find instances of its successful application in practice.

Slum Politics

During the two decades of Congress Party rule, from independence to 1967, little was done to stem the decline of Calcutta. The Basic Development Plan was prepared toward the end of this period, and key decisions were made regarding major infrastructure requirements. Congress strength, however, lay principally in the countryside, and there was little willingness to raise the resources needed to contend with the deteriorating state of the city. Taxation was kept down to the minimum. In the Calcutta Metropolitan Corporation (CMC) corruption and petty politics pushed aside any serious commitment to address the problems of the city. In the late 1960s radical left-wing violence with land-grab origins, known as the Naxilite movement, spread into Calcutta. Political turbulence and fragmentation culminated when West Bengal was placed under presidential rule, with the state governor appointed by New Delhi. There was no return to normal political activity until the 1977 elections, when a communist-dominated coalition known as the Left Front, composed of the Communist Party of India, or CPI (supported by the Soviet Union), the Communist Party of India (Marxist), or CPI(M), and their allies developed strength and handed the Congress Party its first electoral defeat.

The migrant Hindi speakers (as well as the Marwaris from Rajesthan, the Gujaratis, and others from outside Bengal) were already favorably disposed toward Congress when they came to Calcutta, and they still tend to support the party even though it has lost much of its national importance. Congress was strong during the fifties and sixties, and the bustee dwellers voted accordingly. But with industrial decline and a poor economy in the seventies, they increasingly transferred their support to the Left Front.

The core supporters of CPI(M), the key party of the Left Front, are the bustee dwellers and the Calcuttans who trace their origins to the refugees from East Bengal. Largely Bengali, these two groups together constitute as much as half of the city's population. The CPI(M) legalized the bustees and initiated the program of bustee improvement. The incorporation into the CMC of the southern fringe areas of Calcutta with their large refugee populations was done to strengthen this source of support for the ruling CPI(M).[98]

The pressure of Bengali immigration on Calcutta, which has never really let up, has had important political ramifications. Articles appear regularly in the newspapers warning against two contrary threats: "saffronization" on the one hand and "Bangladeshization" on the other. One feeds on the other. Resurgent Hindu nationalism, most alarmingly demonstrated by the 1992 razing of the Ayodhya mosque, augurs dire consequences for the Muslim population, while a flood of illegal Muslim immigration from Bangladesh threatens to subvert India's basic Hindu identity. Ever-growing numbers of Bangladeshis along the eastern border, at its closest point only thirty-five miles from Calcutta, attest to the magnitude of the inflow. They take over the *char* lands that build up from the silt in the river, and many of them (like "illegals" in other countries) are hired as farm laborers because they work for less. Hindu nationalists speak of them as "infiltrators," as distinct from the Hindu immigrants, whom they look upon sympathetically as "refugees," as victims of persecution by a neighboring Islamic state.

Of whatever religion, refugees constitute a ready vote bank to be exploited by local politicians. For five hundred rupees or more, depending on the route, touts on both sides of the border will help them get across, faking medical reports, birth certificates, and ration cards. "Operation Push Back" has been mounted by the Indian Border Security Force in an effort to control this illegal immigration. Muslims are rounded up and evicted, their heads shaved and their transistor radios and other property taken from them as a lesson to others planning to sneak into the country. A wire fence has been put up at the main points of entry along the two-thousand-kilometer border to stem the tide, and also to control smuggling. The issuance of identity cards to West Bengalis as a further control has been under consideration.

In recent years the CPI(M) has lost support among the Bengali middle class. This is partly because of the attention given by the Left Front to the rural areas and its neglect of urban services, and also, it is suggested, because Bengalis are inherently "antiestablishment." Besides, CPI(M) is no longer the party of reform that it was when it took power in 1977. It has become no different from the Congress of earlier days with its goondas and "antisocial" henchmen. The Left Front is now closely linked to the local mafia dons, who are always happy to finance politicians. In the early eighties the party needed their help to deliver the vote, and, as long as they delivered, the dons were immune from police intervention. The Calcutta press thrives on stories of the nexus between politics and crime: for instance, the bomb explosion which demolished three houses in Bowbazar in March 1993, just "a stone's throw" away from the central police headquarters, resulting in many deaths and many wounded and attributed to a "satta don" who had an arsenal of bombs and other weapons and entertained senior police officers with whiskey and women.

Satta is the illegal numbers racket which operates quite openly throughout the city. The "bigwigs" (a typical outmoded English word used in the press to describe anyone in authority) simply look the other way, as they do with the sale of country liquor and other illicit activities. Police officers will pad out their low pay through *tolas,* which they collect from hawkers and from produce and garment sellers for the use of the sidewalks, and from drivers and mechanics for the auto or rickshaw repairs done on the street. Prostitution also offers lucrative opportunities, as a journalist describes from his visit to a brothel:

> [The red-light area of Sobnagach] is well organized but not quite as laid back as it used to be. A quarter of a century ago, I remember the girls had fed us mangoes whilst we waited for our friends. But now everyone is in a hurry. "Either you go in," the man advised me when I went to check the place out, "or go home." The trouble with tarrying apparently is that around 11 P.M. a police party from the nearby station descends on the area and picks up whomever they can. It is beside the point that the two policemen on the beat relax on a cot in harmony with the world till that time. As I said, the place is well organized, because even during the "raid" nobody enters the brothels and word has it that the guys who are picked up, are, well, released for a fee.[99]

Over the many years that it has been in power, the CPI(M) has moved away from its original revolutionary ideology. To attract outside investment in an increasingly free-market environment, the party has comfortably accommodated itself to capitalism. With property values skyrocketing, it is easy to imagine, after all, the close links that exist between party stalwarts, building promoters, and their respective underworld connections. The party cannot afford to take action against promoters who have political influence just to enhance its revolutionary image. So while the police stand aside, still another story is built on top of unsafe foundations, to the point where the entire edifice collapses—with tragic consequences for the people living in the bustee below.

CMDA took over responsibility for urban development in 1971, when West Bengal was under "president's rule" from New Delhi. There was no political participation to speak of at the local level of city borough and ward. The only way to involve the slum dwellers was through appointed bustee advisory committees.

Bustee youth helped install the infrastructure, but decision making and responsibility for its maintenance lay elsewhere. By the time of the 1977 elections, which brought the Left Front to power, it was being openly argued that improving the bustees did not really alter the conditions of the poor but just kept them alive to be exploited as cheap labor. If the poor were to be properly served, a decentralized network of institutions with strong emphasis on elected municipalities was needed. Contrary to initial expectations, little had been accomplished in raising local revenues. Also, responsibility for maintaining newly installed infrastructure had not been transferred to local bodies at anywhere near the rate originally planned. To correct these problems, three laws were passed in 1980 to improve financial management and operations and open up opportunities for new revenues, including a separate fund for bustee maintenance.[100]

In 1982, for the first time in fourteen years, municipal elections were held as the first step in the state government's program to revitalize local governments. The Bustee Improvement Program (BIP) was absorbed within a new Municipal Development Program funded under a World Bank loan. Cash block grants were made to municipalities to be spent for whatever purposes they regarded as important, CMDA serving merely as an overall planning and coordinating body. Choice of investment—be it for water supply, drainage, disposal of solid waste, conversion of "service privies," or improvement of markets—and mobilization of resources through rents and taxes were to be handled by the ward-level authorities. It was argued that municipal board members would be the most concerned with the needs of the poorest citizens, whose support they needed in order to get elected. But it has since turned out that bustee improvement constitutes a small share of the proposals forwarded by municipalities. Just as in the past, the major share of municipal revenues is spent on staff, with little left over for operations and maintenance and nothing for new development.

These changes in how funds were allocated represented a shift in emphasis in favor of the thirty-seven municipalities outside of the Calcutta and Howrah Metropolitan Corporation areas. The outlying areas had been growing more rapidly than the core of the city but had not benefited under the earlier programs, specifically with respect to improvement of bustees where the refugees and migrants lived. Not surprisingly, they were also the areas where Left Front support was strongest.

A mayor-in-council system came into effect at that time. It reestablished the ward councillors as the representatives of the people in the bustees. There are 141 wards in the CMC area, grouped into boroughs, each of which controls a portion of the municipal budget. Direct popular elections every five years decide who will be the councillor in each ward. The councillors then elect seven aldermen, and together they elect the mayor. The mayor selects a deputy and eleven members responsible for specific sectors, one of which is slum improvement and environment.

Decision making was in this way decentralized. During past decades, policy was determined centrally and administered top-down. Now technocrats are subordinate to elected officials, and authority has devolved to the borough and ward levels. Boroughs submit plans to CMC based on local priorities, and funds are allocated accordingly. The boroughs have responsibility for implementing their programs. Because the borough chairman is elected by the ward councillors, there is (in principle) accountability to local interests. There are technical staff posted at the borough level, and health, education, and community development officers sit on the ward committee chaired by the ward councillor. The extent to which the system of delegation operates in practice is hard to say. It seems to work considerably better in those wards where there are strong bustee committees.

But on the ground little has changed. Fiscal discipline remains weak, and the perennial problem of revenue deficits is as serious as ever. Funds are insufficient for the operation and maintenance of bustee infrastructure. It still takes several days to replace a lightbulb or fix a water tap. The hope that decentralization would result in more active community participation and responsibility for maintenance has not been fulfilled. Even if it had, participation alone cannot be expected to offer a panacea. Elected local representatives are unwilling to impose user charges and take other tough revenue measures, and slum dwellers are unmindful of the costs and benefits involved in upgrading their living conditions. Water gets wasted and garbage thrown into the street without any thought being given to the cost of collection.

The Left Front represents a range of different political groups, not all leftist. The main pressures it now faces come from upper- and middle-class interests. After the many years it has been in power, its original commitment to social justice and the moral high ground has become increasingly hard to remember. Lip service is still paid to the needs of the poor, but the lion's share of the budget is used to meet the needs of middle- and upper-income Calcuttans. Only 10 percent of CMDA investment is directly targeted for bustee improvement. The inescapable conclusion is that the horrendous privations endured by slum dwellers are, purely and simply, not regarded as a serious priority. There is little political advantage to be gained from taking up poverty issues. The problems are too entrenched and inclusive to permit focused reactions and politically expedient responses.

"One Bengali makes a poet; two Bengalis make a political party; three Bengalis make two political parties," a wag once remarked. Calcuttans are quick to disparage the established ways of city politics. They will say that while politicians make the right noises, they are, in fact, indifferent to the problems of the poor. The politicians have been corrupted by their connections with the vested interests of the upper and middle class and with the criminal elements that provide them with money and voter support. The voters cannot turn them out because there is no effective opposition. The Congress, feeble and increasingly divided, does not offer a viable alternative. A grass-roots voter revolt would in any case be frustrated by threats and strong-arm tactics. Party cadres would make certain that the voting lines were long enough to discourage concerned citizens from exercising the franchise, or they would obligingly arrange to vote on their behalf. Slum dwellers can be easily manipulated as voter banks by politicians at time of election. Once elections are safely out of the way, there is no reason to show concern for their problems.

The business community is equally unconcerned with the needs of the poor. Calcuttans say that Bengali businessmen are only interested in festivals, cultural events, and displays of influence and political connections. The lighting of the stadium or the construction of a monument receives more of their attention than the resettlement of evicted squatters or the education of street children. Marwaris and other businessmen whose origin is from outside Bengal likewise could care less. Even if they have lived their entire lives in the city, at heart they still do not identify with its problems; their loyalties reside elsewhere.

Urban scholar and member of citizen action groups Raj Kapoor writes that "status seeking, image building, political opportunism, do-gooding in the name of social service . . . constitute the sum total of the motivations behind the actions of the private sector. . . ." He cites the limited results from dialogues between the chamber of commerce, civic groups, and administrative agencies regarding the maintenance of public parks and the construction of public toilets (the kind of image building that could make for adverse publicity).[101]

And as Arthur Row, Ford Foundation consultant, observed:

> It is perhaps ironic, but eminently just, that the Foundation's efforts to move outside government to tap the resources of the larger community should have found their response, not in the elusive business community so long courted, but in the bustee dwellers and the poorly supported voluntary agencies trying to help them. Men from the business community have been . . . involved because of their sensitivity as men, not as members of the business community.[102]

Even when inherent in the culture, do the selfless impulses that find expression in the Calcutta slums only reside in individuals as such, and never in groups, classes, and institutions?

One such dedicated individual is Kanu Babu, secretary of the Jana Seva (People's Service) club and head of a local shop owners' association that was organized to protect small shop owners "from the jaws of local hooligans" and from onerous government taxes. Once a very ill friend of his had to be taken to a hospital. No ambulance was available. Vehicles belonging to the municipality were broken down, and the prices charged by private services out of reach. Kanu Babu pledged on the spot to establish an ambulance service for the poor. With his own money and some funds from local shop owners, he fixed up a second-hand ambulance and arranged credit through the businessmen's association to cover gasoline and maintenance costs (one of the businessmen owned a filling station). He hoped to meet other expenses by providing services to private nursing homes, but they asked for kickbacks. Sidewalk dwellers and squatters pay a few rupees for use of the service. If they cannot pay, they are moved free of charge to a hospital when ill, injured, experiencing a difficult childbirth, or if dying, to Mother Teresa's. No help comes from the well-to-do residents in the neighborhood. As Kanu Babu puts it, they only support religious and cultural events which provide publicity and confer status on the neighborhood.

Understanding the interplay of personalities and factions which takes place at the neighborhood and bustee level remains largely beyond the reach of the outsider. Without intimate knowledge of the principal actors, the outsider must rely on informants, with their individual biases. Without fluent command of the language, key nuances behind what is said are invariably lost.

To a certain extent the political dynamics become more trans-parent in the unimproved bustees in the eastern part of the city. A few years ago these bustees were included in the so-called Cal-cutta Slum Improvement Program supported by British aid. The program differs in degree from the BIP in having a stronger community development component. Infrastructure and sanita-tion improvements include training in simple maintenance, such as clearing drains and repairing pumps. Community development includes preschool and vocational training, as well as sports, folk theater, and other cultural programs, and constitutes a new departure in giving special responsibility to local clubs. The clubs make their premises available for preprimary classes, health awareness, and other programs. They engage the teachers, who are paid an honorarium by the project, and identify beneficiaries to be selected by the ward committee. In return, the project supplies them with books, sports equipment, and financial help in order to expand their facilities. Not all clubs are allowed to participate. Those which are not approved are presumably those which are linked to opposition parties.

The ward committee is chaired by the elected ward councillor and includes bustee and club representatives as well as ex officio representatives of the CMC and technical departments. The ward is divided into *mahallas*, or bustee clusters, of roughly equal population. Each bustee committee elects a representative to the cluster committee, and the cluster committee selects one member to serve as its representative on the ward committee.

Impenetrable to the outsider is the role of the dadas. Ward councillors, when asked, dismiss them as irrelevant. But to enter certain bustees or to interview residents requires the dada's permission, so they obviously have influence. They are usually described as the successors to the zamindars who used to control the area. With their political ties, they collect money from the residents in return for assurances of support on issues of local concern. The customary puja subscriptions *(chanda)*, which they collect mainly from neighboring middle-class households, are an important source of their income. According to the stereotype, they have their own musclemen *(mastan)*, semieducated toughs for whom "party work" is a source of esteem. When picked up by political elements, young men, who would otherwise be a burden on their parents, consider themselves lucky.

At the local level it is the dadas and their henchmen who deliver the votes, by capturing polling booths, stuffing ballot boxes, and clogging the polling stations to discourage others from voting, which is the same thing. In return for these services and for their shadowy mafia connections, they are given license to traffic in *ganga*—marijuana—or country liquor (a potent and illegal rice concoction and the main drug among the poor), or concessions in gambling or prostitution, or the right to sell sidewalk space to hawkers, market women, and indigent migrants. They become part of the the patronage network and many eventually become politicians themselves. After years of service to the party, a loyal dada may be nominated to be ward councillor. A simple majority is all that is needed to be elected. Given the size of the overall bustee community in most wards, in the end it is the bustee residents who determine the outcome. Their choice is not based on ideology or platform but on their immediate everyday needs, which is where the dadas come in.

So the principal actors at the local level are the official ward councillor, the unofficial dadas, and the clubs, bustee committees, and cluster or citizen committees representing several bustees. Somewhat apart are the NGOs, with their separate agendas and funding. They usually try to keep their distance from government and ward committees, which in any case have no matching funds to speak of to support their pet projects. Provided they do not agitate and their projects are not regarded as politically threatening, NGOs can work in the bustees and among squatters and sidewalk dwellers, and the Left Front can take credit for whatever is accomplished.

While some of their activities in craft training and the like are perhaps marginal, NGOs have a beneficial impact in sustaining the vitality of community groups. Bustee committees meet regularly and are held accountable, and agitation for basic entitlements does not let up. This is less likely to happen in the case of committees formed spontaneously around a local resident with political connections. The political party will express interest prior to elections, after which the community is forgotten and its committee loses relevance. In one bustee residents said that the ward councillor does not even bother to show up for meetings.

A community organization which has strong leadership is able to establish close relations with local politicians, police, and influential persons and advance the interests of the bustee or squatter colony. An active bustee committee settles disputes, discusses problems, and through the ward councillor or NGO, proposes solutions. In a squatter settlement, where the main preoccupation is security of tenure, even the Chief Minister of West Bengal may at times see fit to assure residents that their huts will not be demolished. Threats of eviction have mobilized the squatters, just as improvement programs have mobilized bustee dwellers, instilling a feeling of involvement and an element of control over their living conditions. This is most evident in the more recently settled peripheral areas which still maintain some measure of the village pattern, and where political participation is actively encouraged. In the more centrally located bustees, which are becoming more crammed, economically stratified, and politically and ethnically divided, the emergent tensions militate against the ideals of grassroots political consciousness and participation.

The Intractability of Urban Poverty

There is a tendency to treat "the poor" as an undifferentiated mass or as a discrete category that can be studied and analyzed. But failure to disaggregate the poor leads inevitably to generalizations such as "the culture of poverty" or "permanent underclass," which ascribe common traits and convey negative connotations. Poverty then becomes an immutable condition, a trap from which there is no escape.

Even sidewalk dwellers or the homeless, as distinct from other forms of the poor, do not constitute a meaningful category because they include different types of persons with different motivations for making their home on the streets: some with families, others without, some temporary, others more permanently established, some choosing to do so because of convenience to work, others destitute, sick, or disabled who have no other alternative. Thus, too, with bustee dwellers, who must likewise be differentiated: some are families, others are single migrants sharing a room, others are businessmen and shopkeepers, others are scavengers and sweepers; some could afford better accommodations, while others are teetering on the verge of being pushed out and becoming squatters. The squatters themselves are by no means homogeneous. Although many are ragpickers, domestic servants, and beggars, among them are also artisans and regularly paid workers. Then, most hidden from view and difficult to categorize, even to identify for that matter, are the genteel poor, the erstwhile bhadralok families who survive from hand to mouth on fixed rents or other precarious income. They try to maintain a middle-class appearance while barely being able to keep their heads above water.

Defining the poor in terms of "slums" in any generic sense is equally imprecise and inevitably suspect. There is every gradation of slum imaginable, especially in Calcutta, where slums have seeped into the nooks and crannies of the urban landscape and blurred disparities between lower-income and slum housing. Since earliest times, slums have developed wherever there was need of cheap labor and services. Present-day distinctions between them are legalistic and artificial and used mainly for policy convenience. There are the "improved" bustees, where basic services and utilities are available even though they may be irregular and poorly maintained. In some bustees, the physical conditions and amenities are no worse, and often quite better, than are found in decrepit kothabari walk-ups. In others, conditions appall by any standard of human dignity. Then there are the unimproved bustees in the outlying areas where rural attributes hang on, where the air is still fresh and there is space for planting some vegetables, keeping a cow and some chickens. No two bustees are alike: some are inner-city, others semirural; some single-story pockets of moderate density, pleasant to visit; others congested and befouled beyond description; others in the process of blending into the surrounding neighborhood, a mix of low houses with brick walls and, here and there, a mosque or temple and bigger houses with upper stories and balconies.

Bustees were once regarded as the slums of Calcutta, and many of them still merit the stigma. Now the true slums of Calcutta (and other cities) are the illegal squatter settlements, where poverty is unrelieved and the most rudimentary services are absent. These dense jumbles of hovels provide the most glaring expression of utter degradation. But then again, defying generalization, there are some settlements in which squatters have been living for years and enjoy political backing and reasonable security of occupancy.

Not only is each slum unique in its own way, it is also in a continuing state of flux and change. Many slums have been greatly improved. Once improved, they become more crowded and more ethnically diverse. They are less representative of the transfer of rural values into the city. With increasing congestion and pressure to develop centrally located property, they are more urbanized and their residents more integrated into the urban culture. Slums change also when the most vulnerable inhabitants are displaced, as they have been since the earliest days of Calcutta. So also with squatter settlements; they are demolished and new ones spring up, virtually overnight.

In many bustees the environment is deteriorating because of poor maintenance of infrastructure. Bustee improvements were part of a one-shot effort with little follow-up, so hand pumps stay broken, drains and latrines blocked, electric power disrupted. The problem boils down to expanding the extent of private space so that residents assume a collective responsibility instead of depending upon the municipality to correct whatever goes wrong. Poor maintenance is also a function of migrant attitudes and lack of commitment to urban living. Whether a tenant in a rundown bustee or an occupant in a shantytown, the slum dweller who has no assurance of being able to stay put (and who in any case might regard the city only as a temporary abode), has little incentive to take matters in his own hands and better his living conditions.

Municipal attention has focused on improving the microenvironment, less because of any innate humanistic concern than for aesthetic and public health reasons. Bustees were seen as the source of diseases which could spread and threaten all citizens without distinguishing between good and bad neighborhoods. This fear of epidemic—most recently, pneumonic plague—could have a positive outcome if it means extending the minimum amenities of water and sanitation to squatters. It is obvious that legal status alone is insufficient reason to neglect the basic essentials for human dignity. To ignore the public health needs of the those forced to live in such conditions would be, most surely, at everyone's peril.

It is astonishing still to hear the discredited argument that improvements will only encourage more in-migration. Migrants establish footholds in the city through kinsmen and other contacts already established there. Whether they can earn a livelihood determines whether they stay, not the quality of accommodation or the availability of services. Rehabilitation of basic infrastructure does not stimulate more in-migration. Calcutta's core received most attention in terms of basic services delivery to the bustees, yet there has been less in-migration to the central city during the past decade than to the suburban municipalities, which grew at three times the rate without these services.

Without a basic minimum of amenities, however, well-intentioned programs to improve the health and education of residents are seriously compromised. To have lasting effect, practical health training calls for complementary efforts to provide clean water and sanitation, and better classroom instruction requires adequate lighting and ventilation. Physical improvements can also spur informal sector activity and create jobs: electricity allows work to be done at night; access roads bring cars or rickshaws and business into the slum (even though there is a price to pay in terms of noise and pollution).

Had slums developed on vacant public land as in many cities (and leaving aside questions of cost), upgrading could have been handled in a more systematic and comprehensive way. But the three-tier tenure system of Calcutta stood in the way, especially because it denied hut occupants a stake in the process. Improvements could only be stopgap and patch-up and, when done, the bustee was still a slum, albeit a somewhat improved one. A minimum amount of upgrading was the only affordable solution. It inculcated a sense of belonging, however, and while the evidence is inconclusive and opinions will differ, it appears, that, overall, not much displacement of families has taken place. In safeguarding the rights of the intermediate tenants and slumlords, bustee improvement preserved the status quo. It kept the poor in slum pockets but left intact their informal networks and access to work. Better a substandard solution than one which disrupts community life and sweeps the poor into situations in which they enjoy absolutely no rights and services at all.

With rapidly escalating land values, the government came under pressure to regain control of urban land and deal more explicitly with inner-city bustee pockets. This led to legislation which permitted hut owners to make improvements and increase densities. The buildup of slum properties to accommodate more people and the impulse to increase rents has resulted in more displacement and mounting pressure on the services and utilities that at long last had been installed. The living conditions for those who could afford to stay have therefore not always improved as a result of the investments. The threat of rent increases and eviction remains foremost in their minds. In the past, the Left Front encouraged them to stand fast against such threats. Now, because the ideological stance of the Left Front is faltering, tenants can only rely on a process of protracted delay in the courts.

The first slums were established by indigent migrants to provide services and labor to the bhadralok gentry, and over the years migrants have always constituted a vital part of the labor force. When the older generation retired to its villages, a next generation took its place, such as in the tanneries of Tangra-Tiljila or in a Muslim bustee in north Calcutta. It is fair to expect that there will always be migrants because of population pressures, rural distress, and the urban demand for cheap, easily replaceable labor. There will, of course, also be a growing demand for skilled workers, particularly within India's present free-market environment. However, the opportunities open to illiterate migrants from the countryside to improve their skills will be constrained by their abject dependence on low-paying, dead-end jobs with high turnover. Eventually retiring to their villages, unskilled relatives will move in to take their places within the same syndrome that slum conditions inexorably impose.

Rural modernization can help reduce the inflow. Development in the countryside makes life there more attractive, lessens the gap between rural and urban incomes, and improves the rural market for urban goods and services. These changes stimulate urban output and employment, which in turn increase demand for rural production and create jobs. This symbiotic relationship between metropolis and hinterland is therefore often cited as the key to any long-term urban solution. But it has also been pointed out that heavy investment in the rural sector contains "a curious policy paradox: the short-term neglect of Calcutta in favour of rural investment seems to be the only way of ensuring a future for the city in the long term."[103] Besides, even if the huge amount of resources that would be needed became available, there is little reason to expect that rural development will do much to discourage the exodus from the countryside. Rural development involves almost by definition consolidation of holdings and capital investments at the farm level which tend to displace labor. Displaced peasants become the victims of this modernization. It may be that migrants no longer go to the city center as they did in the past but instead to the outlying municipalities which are now growing most rapidly. So urban poverty will continue to spread into the hinterland.

Insofar as Calcutta remains largely a city of migrants, a substantial percentage of the population will have little stake in its future. They will look upon the city as only a place to earn money. They will look upon slum living as a means to better their rural life, choosing to live in a slum, perhaps in shared premises, paying the lowest rent possible, and saving money to invest for other purposes outside. It is therefore unlikely that even enhanced security of tenure will unleash the self-help investments in housing and maintenance of facilities needed to generate spontaneous development. Poverty can be relocated but it will not go away.

The picture is not unrelievedly pessimistic, however. There is a crucial, redeeming element in the urban predicament. The pattern of community migration and settlement and continued economic, social, and cultural attachment to places of origin induce the poor to maintain traditional ways of living and thinking. This distinctive feature of migrant attitudes inserts a vital stabilizing element into the poverty environment. True of all cities, it has special validity in Calcutta, where the picture is one of persistent poverty, not one of social disorganization and alienation.

Caste distinctions are no longer as important as they once were. Even in work considered unclean, castes are coalescing into homogeneous occupational groups which facilitate adjustment to urban life. By providing the psychic moorings with home villages and rural traditions, group sentiment works against anomie and hopelessness. In this respect, urban poverty reinforces traditional values, as expressed in the importance of myths and songs in the lives of slum dwellers. At the same time, the city provides escape from the stigma of caste. It is where the poor can break free from the restraints of their birth. The work they perform provides an essential minimum of self-respect, even if it entails ragpicking and other demeaning activities.

The despair and isolation often found among the poor elsewhere is much less evident in Calcutta. The ragpicker clears the sidewalk on which the family lives, and the stamped clay floor of the most miserable hut is swept regularly. "A desperate cleanliness, wrested from misery," as Gunter Grass called it, epitomizes the urge to live a regular life, whatever the circumstances. This urge engenders the tough resilience that is so much admired among the poor. It is apparent among youngsters living on the railway platform and among women bringing back buckets of water on their heads late at night so as to bathe in the privacy of their windowless trackside shacks. It is inherent in the culture which shields Calcutta's poor against social alienation and the psychological toll of poverty—the erosion of human dignity and self-respect.

With increased congestion, the spread of education, and more intercaste marriage, joint family traditions break down and rural ties weaken. Born and raised in the city, second-generation migrants have less experience with rural life, perhaps none at all. Returning to the countryside may not be an option for many of them. Relationships are restricted increasingly to the city. Institutions with origins in the countryside are supplanted by associations representing urban political interests and sponsors. Bustee committees are formed to support the interventions of government and NGOs. There is increased competition among them for resources from outside traditional mutual help networks.

These changes will ultimately result in a more homogeneous and urbanized slum population, imbued, like the refugees, with a greater sense of commitment to the city. Meanwhile, however, the vestiges of ethnic and caste traditions linger on and find expression in neighborhood pride and, among the older generation, in cherished myths and nostalgia for the past. Residents support a neighborhood temple and continue to worship a particular local deity who taught them a caste vocation they no longer practice. A committee is formed in the squatter settlement as an expression of caste solidarity and for the collection of contributions for festivals. Sidewalk dwellers living in utter privation tenaciously adhere to their social and cultural institutions. In those parts of the city which have not been severed by a major thoroughfare and inundated by outsiders, the enduring presence of traditional groups based on caste infuses a parochial consciousness.

There is nothing moribund or sullen about Calcutta. Even in its architecture, there is little of the drab monotony of other cities. The streets and the sidewalks are a constant bustle of activity, day and night. Turn off the main road into the bustee to find a small world buzzing with life, animated with the shouts and laughter of children and the trading, manufacturing, tinkering, repairing, sorting, carrying, and all the other kinds of work being done. The vitality of the informal sector distinguishes the slums of Calcutta from the "slums of despair" encountered elsewhere. That working conditions are insecure and exploitative does not discount the importance of the informal sector in creating jobs for the poor. Hand picking and sorting through garbage, however repugnant, is appropriate recycling under the conditions. It is ecologically sound and, for the time being at least, provides a livelihood for large numbers of people.

The conditions of work would improve if there were regulations bringing the informal sector within the protection of the law—provided the regulations were enforced. As it is, laws on the books, such as the one restricting the number of hours children may work, are usually ignored. And when they are enforced, it is for negative and punitive purposes: to extract protection money or to curtail the activity of petty traders and workers in cottage industry. Restrictive systems of permits force artisans and traders to operate illegally and rickshaw pullers to pay bribes because their vehicles are unlicensed. As things stand, laws encourage the criminalization of the poor.

On the other hand, the application of uniform technical specifications and quality standards, for whatever good reasons, does not take into account the needs of enterprises operating with little capital, salvaged materials, and simple equipment. It can be argued that the needs of producers and workers in the informal sector must be recognized, with laws and regulations being used as tools of change, as opposed to a means of maintaining the status quo. But to apply this principle and still protect mainstream interests raises difficult issues. Most conventional forms of support, such as vocational training, technical and marketing assistance, even credit without collateral requirements, have little relevance in the informal sector. Lifestyles inherently resistant to change constitute the bulk of activity, and petty services have no demand for technical help.

Besides, there are too many inherent constraints limiting the extent to which the informal sector can be vitalized, not the least of which is the difficulty of dealing with myriad enterprises operating on a very small scale in unregulated and often clandestine markets. In any event, the number of persons who would benefit would constitute a drop in the bucket, compared to the magnitude of the need. In highly competitive markets, restructuring which enhances the productivity of some enterprises can only be done at the expense of others. And when all is said and done, there is no escaping the unpalatable fact that the vitality of the informal sector depends in large measure upon ruthless exploitation of labor.

Resolving the problems of urban poverty entails radical redistribution of resources, hence the solutions are political, not technical. The root problems have to do with how private property is used. Throughout Calcutta's history, since the time when the bhadralok first moved into real estate, it has been property ownership that has driven development. The town was an agent for generating wealth, and for the sake of profit scandalous conditions were tolerated as a means of lowering costs. When land was needed for development, slum dwellers had no choice but to find more crowded accommodations or take to the mudflats. Briefly in the 1970s, there was promise that serious attention would be given to the needs of the poor. However, a government that once identified with the refugees and bustee dwellers became increasingly influenced by property interests, and the way was opened for untrammeled reality speculation. Fundamental problems (which legislation in the early eighties sought to correct) were never really addressed, and the policies that were adopted only served to mitigate the symptoms. Little could be gained in developing "policy solutions" when the whole thrust of development was in the direction of maintaining slum levels of congestion.

The prevailing climate has been one of indifference to poverty, even when the most elementary essentials for human dignity are lacking. Decision makers can neither alienate landowning groups nor throw squatters out without generating public wrath. The best course of action becomes no action at all or ameliorative half measures in deference to the city's fastest-growing constituency. The subject of poverty is too diffuse to allow for concerted political attention. Simply stated, as part of a political agenda, it offers no palpable payoff. It has value mainly in electioneering slogans and in the cornucopia of votes that can be garnered in the slums. Manipulated by politicians and thoroughly politicized, slums are no longer amenable to objective policy solutions.

The private sector has also shown itself to be indifferent to the needs of the poor, in part because the problems are too vast when viewed from the narrow perspective of business interests. There is little evidence of a social responsibility which results in more than occasional almsgiving to worthy causes. Moreover, the Bengali community, which by rights should be the most concerned, has lost out to Marwaris and other outsiders who do not identify with the city. The conclusion that businesses are only interested in prestige projects and short-term palliatives having symbolic importance becomes inescapable.

There is, on the other hand, a wellspring of charitable concern and capacity on the part of individuals and neighborhood groups. It is seen in the dedication of ex-bureaucrats who devote their retirement years to working in the slums, and in the modest offices of social agencies, where a room may be given over to classes for street children. But mobilizing this potential on the wide scale that is needed has proven to be difficult. How to manage the vested interests of the various civic groups and their political patrons and orchestrate their dispersed interventions so that they are complementary and supportive and not working at cross-purposes? And how to channel financing into their activities without discouraging resourcefulness or smothering individual autonomy and initiative? NGOs have their separate clienteles, agendas, and sources of funding, which they jealously guard. Their priorities are based to an extent on the perceptions of outsiders, which are not always in accord with the felt needs of the communities they ostensibly serve. Their emphasis on empowerment and the rights of the poor (ragpickers, prostitutes, children, etc.) is to be applauded in that it gets at the roots of poverty. Their real strength lies in their flexibility and innovativeness and in the dedication of their staff. However, a jealous independence acts to the detriment of the overall impact of what they are doing. Accomplishments tend to be marginal and scattered because of an unwillingness to conform to any overarching program approach and control. In the end, there is a serious problem of scale.

Addressing the needs of slum pockets in isolation, which is the preference of aid donors and NGOs, has limited effectiveness. Programs that ameliorate conditions can also do harm by creating inequities and dissensions and by helping some people at the expense of others. Politicians thrive in these conditions, which further politicize the slums. They draw invidious comparisons between improved and unimproved areas and attention to interrupted projects and unfulfilled promises. Also, many slums are no longer discrete pockets of poverty representing rural patterns and lifestyles. They have infested all parts of the city, wherever there are decrepit buildings that are no longer being kept up, older houses turned into clotted tenements, bustees where utilities are not properly maintained, insanitary cattle sheds with their attendant swarms of flies, and grotesque colonies of squatters huddled on sidewalks, under bridges, and along railroads and canals. Mainstream society cannot have the convenience of cheap labor without slums intruding visibly into the interstices of urban space. Not only Calcutta but all major cities in India are half slums already, and the evidence is incontrovertible that the rate of growth of slums is faster than the growth of the city as a whole. Calcutta's advantage is its pervasive awareness of poverty; it is still a city above pretense. Whereas in the West, poverty is seen by the not-so-poor only at a distance, on television, or from the suburbs, or through the car window when driving by the graffiti, the boarded-up buildings, the empty, rubble-strewn lots. "Slum, semi-slum and superslum—to this has come the evolution of cities."[104]

It is easy to become fatalistic. "The poor ye shall always have with you." But if forced to find answers, they will be found in policies based on a positive approach toward the urban poor. At least in the short run, policies must accept the fact that the poor are an intrinsic part of the city, even more as ethnic and rural ties weaken. Showing admirable initiative and ingenuity, the poor are doing their best to cope. They should be helped in finding their own solutions. With regard to the informal sector, this calls for toleration and noninterference, benign neglect if you will, not suppression, in order to provide the stability needed for spontaneous self-help and a thriving small-scale economy. Policies should recognize that there are efficiencies in the bustle and congestion of street trading and hawking besides providing livelihoods for large numbers of people.

The experience of Calcutta suggests the need to adopt an "austerity model"[105] in providing services to the poor. The only sustainable interventions are those which make optimum use of whatever resources exist in the slum community. The only meaningful training is the training of workers from the community as paramedics, nutritionists, or literacy educators without detaching them from their roots. The low-cost health services provided by "honorary health workers" are a fine example of this. Flexible teaching arrangements which offer at least some education, even if plainly deficient, to children who have no choice but to work during the daytime also make eminent sense. Whatever exists should be used and not jettisoned and replaced with facilities and services from outside. Maximum reliance should be placed on youth clubs and people's organizations rather than on external agencies with their high overheads and superannuated officials. Low-tech, environmentally appropriate solutions with regard to transport and garbage recycling should be accorded respectability, especially in view of automobile pollution and the growing demand for recycled materials. More flexible standards should be adopted. Water supplies are now based on two hundred liters a day per person being piped to the wealthier quarters, while the poor rely on communal standpipes with intermittent pressure or on water vendors who charge extortionist rates. Free milk is distributed to slum kids on the basis of some arbitrary standard (probably what a middle-class, well-fed American child needs), rather than the amount that can be consumed without becoming contaminated under slum conditions. Urban land policy and zoning strategies push up densities and land values in the very areas where the poorest people must make their living. Traffic policies accommodate the needs of the affluent, car-owning minority, rather than those of the pedestrians, street vendors, rickshaw pullers, and handcart owners. Urban roads should not be the subject of traffic management schemes alone, given their widespread use by the poor for residential and commercial purposes.

It would be naïve, however, to believe that such a model, valid as it may be in theory, would meet with general approval. It would be opposed by developers and proponents of city beautification and free-flowing traffic. Any lowering of standards and denial of established norms and optimum solutions would be professionally untenable. Knowing on which side their bread is buttered, planners would reject the notion that slum dwellers are more qualified than trained specialists to work out the answers to their problems or that a composite of their localized plans would be better than any "rationalized" bureaucratic solution. It would violate conventional adherence to quality standards and institutions and the inevitability of progress. It would refute the premise that poverty can be eradicated. Planning cities for the poor would be considered tantamount to an admission of failure. Moreover, it would most surely incur the opposition of middle-class and property interests, which no politician can afford to ignore. Adopting the austerity model would imply the rejection of more palatable and congenial scenarios (however problematical they may be): That rural investment and improved conditions in the countryside with its impoverished millions can, in fact, reduce pressures on the city; that capital investment and a dynamic urban economy will create jobs and reduce levels of poverty (burgeoning slum populations in booming cities such as Bombay notwithstanding).

Instead, to face up to social reality, the needs of the poor must take a central place in urban policy. The poor cannot be treated as an afterthought, or shunted off to some department or other, or left to rely on the benevolence of NGOs and the private sector. Conditions must be created which help them work out their own solutions, knowing that only through their own efforts and resources under their own control will they make the political structure respond to their needs. As long as these conditions are absent, the blight of urban poverty will remain as intractable as ever.

Notes

1. Norton Ginsburg, review of Harold Lubell's book in *Economic Development and Cultural Change*, pp. 779–780.

2. Soumyendra Nath Mukherjee, *Calcutta: Myths and History*, p. 89.

3. Quotations from John Hutnick, "Calcutta: Poverty as a Tourist Attraction."

4. Chidananda Das Gupta, "Whose City Is It Anyway?" (Calcutta), September 4, 1992.

5. Shashi Tharoor, as quoted in *Telegraph* (Calcutta), April 26, 1992.

6. Sales and Display Publications, Seminar on Calcutta and Its Problems: *Calcutta Today: A Comprehensive Survey*, p. 3.

7. Rudyard Kipling, "A Tale of Two Cities." *Poems*, p. 230.

8. P. Thankappan Nair, *Calcutta in the 18th Century*, p. 277

9. Quotations are from H.E.A. Cotton, *Calcutta Old and New*, pp. 196–197; P. Thankappan Nair, *Calcutta in the 19th Century (Company's Days)*, p. 354.

10. Rev. Howard Malcom, "Travels in South-Eastern Asia"; Nair, *Calcutta in 19th Century*, pp. 782–783.

11. N.K. Ray, *A Short History of Calcutta: Town and Suburbs*, pp. 195–196; Pradip Sinha, "The Genesis of a Colonial City," p. 6.

12. Nair, *Calcutta in the 19th Century*, pp. 580–581.

13. Letters quoted in Ranabira Ray Choudhury, *Calcutta: A Hundred Years Ago*, pp. 112–182.

14. Sumanta Banerjee, *The Parlour and the Streets: Elite and Popular Culture in Nineteenth Century Calcutta*, p. 34; and Anil Ranjan Biswas, *Calcutta and Calcuttans: From Dihi to Megalopolis*, p. 397, quoting a statement of the Marquess of Hastings in 1813.

15. Pradip Sinha, *Calcutta in Urban History*, pp. 8–9.

16. Rabindranath Tagore, as quoted in *Calcutta Municipal Gazetter 1924–47* (Calcutta: Calcutta Municipal Corporation, 1980), p. 21.
17. Rev. James Long, *Calcutta in Olden Times: Its Localities and Its People*, p. 83
18. P. Sinha, *Urban History*, p. 98.
19. See Nirmal Kumar Bose, *Calcutta: A Social Survey, 1964;* also N.K. Bose, "Calcutta: Premature Metropolis."
20. Sumanta Banerjee, "The World of Ramjan Ostagar, the Common Man of Old Calcutta"; S.N. Mukherjee, *Myths and History*, pp. 28–29
21. Rajat Ray, *Urban Roots of Indian Nationalism: Pressure Groups and Conflicts of Interest in Calcutta City Politics, 1875–1939*, p. 89. Tanika Sarkar, *Bengal, 1928–1934: The Politics of Protest*, pp. 101–104.
22. S. Banerjee, "Ramjan Ostagar," pp. 81–82; see also S. Banerjee, *Parlour and Streets*, and Prajnananda Banerjee, *Calcutta and Its Hinterland: A Study in the Economic History of India, 1833–1900*, on which many of these observations are based.
23. As quoted in P. Sinha, *Urban History*, pp. 223–224.
24. Nirad C. Chaudhuri, *The Autobiography of an Unknown Indian*, pp. 380–381.
25. See Geoffrey Moorhouse, *Calcutta*, pp. 66–71.
26. See Narendra Goyal, ed., *The City in Turmoil: Report of a National Seminar;* also Prafulla K. Chakrabarti, *The Marginal Men: The Refugees and the Left Political Syndrome in West Bengal*, pp. 417–418.
27. N.C. Chaudhuri, *Unknown Indian*, pp. 266–267.
28. P. Sinha, *Urban History*, pp. 261–262.
29. See especially N.K. Bose, *Social Survey*, and Saurenda Nath Sen, *The City of Calcutta: A Socio-Economic Survey, 1955–56.*
30. As quoted in Kali Charan Ghosh, *Famines in Bengal 1770–1943*, p. 122; see also Tarak Chandra Das, *Bengal Famine (1943) as Revealed in a Survey of the Destitutes in Calcutta.*
31. Kanti B. Pakrasi, *The Uprooted: A Sociological Study of the Refugees of West Bengal, India*, pp. 83–122. Sixty-eight percent of the refugees settled in Calcutta and the adjacent districts.
32. See Saroj Chakrabarty, *My Years with B.C. Roy: A Record up to 1962*, pp. 89–90.
33. P.K. Chakraburti, *Marginal Men*, p. 13.
34. See Cotton, *Old and New*, pp. 230ff. The poem "This Calcutta and My Lonely Bed," by Samsher Anwar in Surajit Sinha, ed., *Cultural Profile of Calcutta*, p. 168, reflects the insecurities of city life for the refugee; see also Sunil Gangopadhyay, *Arjun*, about life in a refugee colony.
35. See R.M. Kapoor, and M.S. Maitra: *The Marginal Land Owners in Low Income Housing Settlements.*
36. Sarat Chandra as quoted in Sarkar, *Bengal*, p. 63.
37. See Dipesh Chakrabarty, *Rethinking Working Class History: Bengal, 1890–1940.*
38. R. Ray, *Urban Roots*, p. 51.

39. Jean Racine, ed., *Calcutta 1981: The City, Its Crisis and the Debate on Urban Planning and Development*, p. 233.

40. See N. Vijay Jagannathan and Animash Halder, "A Case Study of Pavement Dwellers in Calcutta"; other observations regarding the sidewalk dwellers are drawn from two studies by Sudhendu Mukherjee, *Under the Shadow of the Metropolis: They Are Citizens Too* and *The Sinews of the Informal Sector Economy*.

41. Amitar Ghosh, *The Shadow Lines*, p. 131.

42. These figures are from N.K. Ray, *Short History*, p. 142, and from Murari Ghosh, Alok K. Dutta, and Biswanath Ray; *Calcutta: A Study of Urban Growth Dynamics*, p. 76

43. See Abhijit Dasgupta et al., *A Paper on Urban Reconstruction and Marginalisation*.

44. Philip Appleman, *The Silent Explosion*, p. 3.

45. Nilanjana Chatterjee, "The East Bengal Refugees: A Lesson in Survival," p. 73.

46. Asok Sen, *Life and Labour in a Squatter Colony*, pp. 28–32.

47. Christine Furedy, "Whose Responsibility? Dilemmas of Calcutta's Bustee Policy in the Nineteenth Century," p. 29.

48. Unnayan (Progress), *Basti Movement in Calcutta: Housing Struggle of Basti Dwellers in the 1950's in Calcutta*, p. 10.

49. Survey results from the 1950s are from S.N. Sen, *Socio-Economic Survey*, pp. 259–269. In 1979–1980, the Calcutta Metropolitan Development Authority (CMDA) in collaboration with Team Consultants Private Limited, Calcutta, conducted a socioeconomic survey of 14 bustees. This was followed up more recently by a CMDA study entitled *Slumdwellers of Calcutta: Socio-Economic Profile—1989–90*, by Asok M. Chakrabarti (secretary, CMDA) and Animesh Halder (deputy director, CMDA), covering 19 bustees, which excluded some of the slums in the earlier survey "because the character of the settlements had undergone considerable changes in the intervening period" and included some new slums.

50. These observations are from Center for Research in the Epidemiology of Disasters (Catholic University of Louvain) and the Council for Social Development (New Delhi), *Bustees: Calcutta's Second City: A Study of Access to Health and Nutrition*, pp. 197–263. The 1992 study included improved as well as partly improved bustees and refugee colonies. Squatter settlements were excluded because of the absence of reliable data for sampling purposes.

51. See Dixshit Sinha, "Life in a Calcutta Slum," which describes a Bengali bustee in south Calcutta.

52. As quoted in S. Sengupta, "The Hela Caste in Calcutta," p. 245.

53. Sanjay K. Roy, "Life in Calcutta Slums," p. 67.

54. Dominique Lapierre, *The City of Joy*, pp. 45, 139–140.

55. Furedy, "Whose Responsibility?" p. 19.

56. S.W. Goode, *Municipal Calcutta: Its Institutions in Their Origin and Growth*, pp. 265–271.

57. Ibid., p. 168.

58. R. Ray, *Urban Roots*, pp. 45–48.

59. As quoted in S.B. Ray, "A Massive Attack on Bustees," p. 78.

60. Furedy, "Whose Responsibility?" p. 33.

61. As quoted in ibid., p. 96.

62. Arthur T. Row, *An Evaluation of the Calcutta Planning and Development Project 1961–1974*, pp. 41–42.

63. Sudhendu Mukherjee, *Shelter for the Poor in Calcutta: The Myth and the Reality*, p. 12.

64. Swati Ghosh, *Thika Tenancy in Bustees of Calcutta*, pp. 10–13.

65. Calcutta Municipal Corporation, Committee Report of June 1992, mimeo.

66. K.C. Sivaramakrishnan, "Slum Improvement in Calcutta."

67. Biswas, *Dihi to Megapolis*, p. 6; Cotton, *Old and New*, p. 207.

68. S. Banerjee, *The Parlour and Streets*, pp. 24–26.

69. Hitesranjan Sanyal, *Social Mobility in Bengal*, pp. 50–57, 100–108.

70. Unnayan, *Rickshaws in Calcutta*, p. 2. Lapierre points out that because no licenses have been issued since 1949, there are officially fewer than 10,000 hand rickshaws, but unofficial statistics suggest five times that number. A total of 50,000 would thus provide a living for 100,000 pullers, in addition to others who do repairs and maintenance. Lapierre, *City of Joy*, p. 102.

71. Asok Mitra, "Calcutta's Backyard: 1. Health and Welfare from Garbage," p. 48; see also, N. Vijay, Jagannathan, *Informal Markets in Developing Countries*.

72. The quote is from Paul Theroux, *The Great Railway Bazaar*, p. 176; see also Christine Furedy and Mohammed Alamgir, "Street Pickers in Calcutta Slums."

73. Quotations are from Sanjay K. Roy, "Life in Calcutta Slums," pp. 69–70.

74. *Telegraph* (Calcutta), December 15, 1990, as excerpted from Raghab Bandyophyay, "The Inheritors: Slum and Pavement Life in Calcutta."

75. CMDA *A Study Report on Clay Modellers Community at Kumartuli in Calcutta*, p. 15.

76. Anjana Roy Chaudhury, "Caste and Occupation in Bhowanipur, Calcutta," p. 217.

77. N.K. Bose, "Premature Metropolis," pp. 97–98. Also noted by Subhankar Roy, "The Kansa Baniks of Simla Para, Calcutta." Roy kindly introduced me to Simlapara in 1994.

78. See Asok Sen, *The Bindery Workers of Daftaripara*.

79. A.R. Chaudhury, "Caste and Occupation," pp. 219–220.

80. Robert D. Kaplan, "The Coming Anarchy," p. 64.

81. A.R. Chaudhury, "Caste and Occupation," p. 77.

82. As quoted in S. Banerjee, "Ramjan Ostagar," p. 77. Banerjee writes that it is a pity we do not have a Bengali equivalent of Henry Mayhew's *London Labour and London Poor*, with its fascinating descriptions of the trades and occupations in mid-nineteenth-century London.

83. Sivaramakrishnan, "Slum Improvement in Calcutta," p. 114.

84. Nirmala Banerjee, "Survival of the Poor," pp. 184–185.

85. R. Ray, *Urban Roots,* p. 51

86. See Harold Lubell, *Calcutta: Its Urban Development and Employment Prospects.*

87. See N. Vijay Jagannathan, "Economic Aspects of Calcutta's Basic Development Plan." This picture could readily change if recent efforts by the West Bengal government to encourage private foreign investment in the metropolitan area meet with success.

88. N. Banerjee, "Survival of the Poor," p. 177–178.

89. See Ajit N. Bose, *Calcutta and Rural Bengal: Small Sector Symbiosis,* pp. 103–105.

90. See Harold Lubell and S.V. Sethuraman, *Income and Employment Generating Policies for Lower Income Urban Settlements.*

91. N. Banerjee, "Survival of the Poor," pp. 182.

92. Ibid., p. 183.

93. See World Bank, *Project Performance Audit Report: India First Calcutta Urban Development Project.*

94. Sudhendu Mukherjee, *Typology of Slum and Squatter Settlements in the Metropolis.*

95. See Richard Heaver, *Improving Family Planning, Health and Nutrition Outreach in India: Experience from Some World Bank Assisted Programs.*

96. WHO evaluation, September 1991.

97. From the files of FOCUS (Forum for Communities United in Service), Calcutta.

98. See Atul Kohli, *Democracy and Discontent: India's Growing Crisis of Governability.*

99. A.J.B. Singh, "Under Cover of the Night," *Telegraph* (Calcutta).

100. Bengal Municipal (Amendment) Act, Calcutta Municipal Corporation Act, and Howrah Municipal Corporation Act.

101. R.M. Kapoor, *Sustainable Development of Mega-Cities in Asia: Some Innovative Experiences from Calcutta,* pp. 13–15.

102. Row, *Planning and Development,* p. 28.

103. Omkar Goswani, "Calcutta's Economy, 1918–1970: The Fall from Grace," p. 96.

104. Patrick Geddes, as quoted in Lewis Mumford, *The City in History,* p. 464.

105. A.N. Bose introduced this term to me in a 1993 conversation.

Bibliography

Ali, Hasan. "The Chinese in Calcutta." In M.K.A. Siddigui, ed., *Aspects of Society and Culture in Calcutta*. Calcutta: Anthropological Survey of India, 1982.

Appleman, Philip. *The Silent Explosion*. Boston: Beacon Press, 1965.

Bandyophyay, Raghab. "The Inheritors: Slum and Pavement Life in Calcutta." In Sukanda Chaudhuri, ed., *Calcutta: The Living City*, vol. II, pp. 78–87. Calcutta: Oxford University Press, 1990.

Banerjee, Nirmala. "Survival of the Poor." In Helen I. Safa, ed., *Towards a Political Economy of Urbanization in Third World Countries*. Delhi: Oxford University Press, 1982.

———. *Women Workers in the Unorganized Sector: The Calcutta Experience*. Hyderabad/Calcutta: Orient Longman, 1985.

Banerjee, Prajnananda. *Calcutta and Its Hinterland: A Study in the Economic History of India, 1833–1900*. Calcutta: Progressive, 1975.

Banerjee, Sumanta. *The Parlour and the Streets: Elite and Popular Culture in Nineteenth Century Calcutta*. Calcutta: Seagull Books, 1989.

———. "The World of Ramjan Ostagar, the Common Man of Old Calcutta." In *Calcutta: The Living City*, vol. I, pp. 76–84. Calcutta: Oxford University Press, 1990.

Bhattacharya, K.P. *A Study on Squatter Settlements in Calcutta*. Calcutta: Centre for Human Settlements International, 1962.

Bhattacharya, K.P., and P. Dey. *Problems of Hawkers in Metropolitan Cities: A Case Study of Calcutta*. Occasional Paper no. 2. Calcutta: Centre for Human Settlements International, n.d.

Bhattacharya, Mohit. "Municipal Calcutta and Evolutionary Perspective." In *Calcutta's Urban Future*. Calcutta: West Bengal Government, 1991.

Bhattacharya, Mohit, M.M. Singh, and Frank J. Tysen. *Government in Metropolitan Calcutta.* New York: Institute of Public Administration, 1965.

Biswas, Anil Ranjan. *Calcutta and Calcuttans: From Dihi to Megalopolis.* Calcutta: Firma KLM, 1992.

Blechynden, Kathleen. *Calcutta: Past and Present,* ed. N.R. Ray. Calcutta, 1978.

Bose, Ajit N. *The Informal Sector in the Economy of Metropolitan Calcutta,* World Employment Programme research working paper WEP 2–12/WP 5. Geneva: International Labour Office, October 1974.

————. *Calcutta and Rural Bengal: Small Sector Symbiosis.* Calcutta: Minerva, 1978.

Bose, Nirmal Kumar. "Some Aspects of Caste in Bengal." *Man in India,* June 1958, pp. 73–97.

————. "Modern Bengal." *Man in India.* December 1958, pp. 229–295.

————. "Social and Cultural Life of Calcutta." *Geographical Review of India,* December 1958, pp. 1–46.

————. "Calcutta: Premature Metropolis." *Scientific American,* September 1965, pp. 91–102.

————. *Calcutta: A Social Survey, 1964.* Bombay: Lalvani, 1968.

Broomfield, J.H. *Elite Conflict in a Plural Society: Twentieth Century Bengal.* Berkeley and Los Angeles: University of California Press, 1968.

Center for Research in the Epidemiology of Disasters (Catholic University of Louvain) and the Council for Social Development (New Delhi). *Bustees: Calcutta's Second City: A Study of Access to Health and Nutrition,* ed. Prodipto Roy. New Delhi: Council for Social Development, 1992. Mimeo.

Chakrabarti, Asok M., and Animesh Halder. *Slumdwellers of Calcutta: Socio-Economic Profile—1989–90.* Calcutta: CMDA, 1991.

Chakrabarty, Dipesh. *Rethinking Working Class History: Bengal, 1890–1940.* Princeton, N.J.: Princeton University Press, 1989.

Chakrabarty, Prafulla K. *The Marginal Men: The Refugees and the Left Political Syndrome in West Bengal.* Calcutta: Lumière Books, 1990.

Chakrabarty, Saroj. *My Years with B.C. Roy: A Record up to 1962.* Calcutta: S. Chakrabarty, 1982.

Chatterjee, Nilanjana. "The East Bengal Refugees: A Lesson in Survival." In Sukanda Chaudhuri, ed., *Calcutta: The Living City,* vol. II, pp. 70–77. Calcutta: Oxford University Press, 1990.

Chaudhuri, Keshab. *Calcutta: Story of Its Government.* Bombay: Orient Longman, 1973.

Chaudhuri, Manoranjan. *The Industrial Landscape of West Bengal.* Calcutta and Oxford: IBH, 1971.

Chaudhuri, Nirad C. *The Autobiography of an Unknown Indian.* Berkeley and Los Angeles: University of California Press, 1968.

Chaudhury, Anjana Roy. "Caste and Occupation in Bhowanipur, Calcutta." *Man in India,* 44, no. 2 (1964), pp. 207–220.

Chaudhury, Pradip, and Abhijit Mukherjee. *Calcutta People and Empire: Collection from Old Journals.* Calcutta: India Book Exchange, 1975.

Choudhury, Ranabira Ray. *Calcutta: A Hundred Years Ago.* Bombay: Nachiketa Publications, 1988.

CMDA (Calcutta Metropolitan Development Authority). *Basic Development Plan for the Calcutta Metropolitan District, 1966–86.* Calcutta: Calcutta Metropolitan Planning Organization (CMPO), 1966.

———. *A Study Report on Clay Modellers Community at Kumartuli in Calcutta.* Report no. 47, June 1977.

———. *Socio-Economic Survey in Bustees of Calcutta.* Executive summary, 1980.

———. *Bustee Improvement Programme of CMDA: An Evaluative Study,* 1981.

———. *Calcutta Slums: The Problem and Effort,* 1981.

———. *Shelter Programme and Perspective: CMDA,* 1982.

———. *Report on Health and Socio-Economic Survey,* March 1983.

Cotton, H.E.A. *Calcutta Old and New,* 1909; 2nd ed., Calcutta: N.R. Ray, 1980.

Danda, Ajit. "Socio-Economic Profile of a Calcutta Slum." In Council for Social Development and Ramakrishna Mission, *Symposium on Urbanization and Slums, April 26–28, 1993.* New Delhi, 1993.

Das, Tarak Chandra. *Bengal Famine (1943) As Revealed in a Survey of the Destitutes in Calcutta.* Calcutta: University of Calcutta, 1949.

Das Gupta, Chidananda. "Whose City Is it Anyway?" *The Statesman* (Calcutta), September 4, 1992.

Dasgupta, Abhijit, Nishith Ranjan, Sumitra Dasgupta, and Nita Shirali. "A Paper on Urban Reconstruction and Marginalisation. Calcutta, June 1988. Unpublished manuscript.

Dasgupta, Anil Chandra, ed. *The Days of John Company: Selections from Calcutta Gazette 1824–1832.* Calcutta: Government Printing, 1959.

Dasgupta, Biplab. *Calcutta's Informal Sector.* Bulletin 5. Institute of Development Studies, Sussex, 1973

De Souza, Alfred, ed. *The Indian City: Poverty, Ecology, and Urban Development.* New Delhi: South Asia Books, 1977.

De Souza, Alfred, and Andrea Menefee Singh. *The Urban Poor: Slum and Pavement Dwellers in the Major Cities of India.* New Delhi: Manobar, 1980.

Furedy, Christine. "Whose Responsibility? Dilemma of Calcutta's Bustee Policy in the Nineteenth Century." *South Asia (NS),* 5, no. 2 (1982), pp. 24–46.

Furedy, Christine, and Mohammed Alamgir. "Street Pickers in Calcutta Slums," *Environment and Urbanization,* 4, no. 2 (October 1992), pp. 54–59.

Gangopadhyaya, Sunil. *Arjun.* Calcutta: Ananda, 1971. Reprint, New Delhi: Penguin, 1987.

Ghose, Murari. *Metropolitan Calcutta: Economics of Growth.* Calcutta: OPS, 1983.

Ghosh, Amitar. *The Shadow Lines.* New York: Penguin, 1990.

———. *Street Children of Calcutta.* New Delhi: National Labour Institute, July 1992.

Ghosh, Kali Charan. *Famines in Bengal, 1770–1943.* 2nd ed. Calcutta: National Council of Education, 1987.

Ghosh, Murari, Alok K. Dutta, and Biswanath Ray. *Calcutta: A Study of Urban Growth Dynamics.* Calcutta: K.L. Mukhopadhyay, 1972.

Ghosh, Swati. *Thika Tenancy in Bustees of Calcutta.* Calcutta: Centre for Urban Economic Studies, Calcutta University, 1992.

Ginsburg, Norton. Review of Harold Lubell's book in *Economic Development and Cultural Change,* 25, no. 4 (July 1977), pp. 779–785.

Goode, S.W. *Municipal Calcutta: Its Institutions in Their Origin and Growth.* Edinburgh 1916. Reprint, Calcutta: Bibhash Gupta, 1986.

Goswani, Omkar. "Calcutta's Economy 1918–1970: The Fall from Grace." In Sukanda Chaudhuri, ed., *Calcutta: The Living City,* vol. II, pp. 88–96. Calcutta: Oxford University Press, 1990.

Government of West Bengal, State Statistical Bureau. *Survey of Bustees in Calcutta City, 1958–59.* Calcutta, 1960.

Goyal, Narendra, ed. *The City in Turmoil: Report of a National Seminar.* New Delhi: Gandhi Peace Foundation, 1971.

Grass, Günter. *Show Your Tongue.* New York and London: Harcourt Brace Jovanovitch, 1989.

Guha, Meera. "Social Institutions in a Municipal Ward in Calcutta." *Man in India,* 42, no. 3 (1962), pp. 181–194.

Heaver, Richard. *Improving Family Planning, Health and Nutrition Outreach in India: Experience from Some World Bank Assisted Programs.* Paper prepared for the World Bank. New Delhi, January 1989.

Hutnick, John. "Calcutta: Poverty as a Tourist Attraction," *The Statesman* (Calcutta), September 4, 1992.

Iftikar-ul-Awwal, A.Z.M. *The Industrial Development of Bengal, 1900–1939.* Delhi: Vikas, 1982.

ILGUS (Institute of Local Government and Urban Studies). *Urban Poverty and Policy.* Regional seminar. Calcutta, May 1989.

Indian Chamber of Commerce. *Towards a Better Calcutta: Proceedings of a Seminar Held in April 1965.* Calcutta, 1965.

Jagannathan, N. Vijay. "Economic Aspects of Calcutta's Basic Development Plan." In *Calcutta's Basic Development Plan: In Retrospect.* Calcutta: CMDA and New Delhi: NIUA (National Institute of Urban Affairs), December 1986.

———. *Informal Markets in Developing Countries.* New York: Oxford University Press, 1987.

Jagannathan, N. Vijay, and Animesh Halder. "Income-Housing Linkages: A Case Study of Pavement Dwellers in Calcutta." In *International Seminar on Income and Housing in Third World Urban Development,* New Delhi, November–December 1987.

———. "A Case Study of Pavement Dwellers in Calcutta." *Economic and Political Weekly* (New Delhi) June 4, 1988, pp. 1175–1178, December 3, 1988, pp. 2602–2605, and February 11, 1989, pp. 315–318.

Kahnert, Friedrich. *The Small-Scale Enterprise Credit Program: An Assessment.* Internal discussion paper. Washington, D.C.: World Bank, March 1989.

Kapoor, R.M. *Sustainable Development of Mega-Cities in Asia: Some Innova-

tive Experiences from Calcutta. Report to the Mega-Cities Project. Calcutta: Times Research Foundation, May 1992.

Kapoor, R.M., and M.S. Maitra. *Slums, Squatter Settlements, and Organized Sector Worker Housing in India*. Calcutta: Times Research Foundation, June 1987.

——. *The Marginal Land Owners in Low Income Housing Settlements*. Calcutta: Times Research Foundation, November 1987.

Kipling, Rudyard. "The City of Dreadful Night." In *From Sea to Sea: Letters of Travel*, pp. 185–247. New York: Doubleday, Page and Co., 1920.

——. "A Tale of Two Cities." In Nathan H. Dale, ed., *Poems of Rudyard Kipling*, pp. 229–233. New York: Thomas Crowell, 1888.

Kohli, Atul. *Democracy and Discontent: India's Growing Crisis of Governability*. Cambridge and New York: Cambridge University Press, 1991.

Lapierre, Dominique. *The City of Joy*. New York: Warner Books, 1985.

Long, (Rev.) James. *Calcutta and Its Neighbourhoods: History of the People and Localities from 1670 to 1857*. Calcutta: Granthan, 1974.

——. *Calcutta in Olden Times: Its Localities and Its People*. 1864. Reprint, Calcutta, 1974.

Losty, Jeremiah P. *Calcutta: A City of Palaces: A Survey of the City in the Days of the East India Company, 1690–1858*. London: British Library, 1990.

Lubell, Harold. *Calcutta: Its Urban Development and Employment Prospects*. Geneva: International Labour Office, 1974.

Lubell, Harold, and S.V. Sethuraman. *Income and Employment Generating Policies for Lower Income Urban Settlements*. New York: UN Centre for Housing, Building, and Planning, 1977.

Maitra, M.S. "An Overview on Shelter." In *Calcutta's Basic Development Plan: In Retrospect*. Calcutta: CMDA and New Delhi: NIUA, 1986.

——. "Shelter: Slums and Squatter Settlements." In *Calcutta's Urban Future*. Calcutta: West Bengal Government, 1991, pp. 207–238.

Menezes, Braz O. "Calcutta, India: Conflict or Consistency?" In John P. Lea and John M. Courtney, eds., *Cities in Conflict*. Washington, D.C.: World Bank, 1985.

Mitra, Asok. *Calcutta, India's City*. Calcutta: New Age, 1963.

——. *Calcutta Diary*. Calcutta: Rupa, 1979.

——. "Calcutta's Backyard: 1. Health and Welfare from Garbage." *The Statesman* (Calcutta) January 24, 1984.

Moitra, M.K., and S. Samajdar. "Evaluation of the Slum Improvement Program of the Calcutta Bustees." In UNHCS, *Shelter Upgrading for the Urban Poor,* ed. R.J. Skinner, J.L. Taylor, and E.A. Wegelin. Manila: Island, 1987.

Moorhouse, Geoffrey. *Calcutta*. New York: Holt, Rinehart and Winston, 1971.

Mukherjee, Soumyendra Nath. *Calcutta: Myths and History*. Calcutta: Subarnarekha, 1977.

Mukherjee, Sudhendu. *The Sinews of the Informal Sector Economy*. Calcutta: CMDA, n.d. Mimeo.

——. *Under the Shadow of the Metropolis: They Are Citizens Too*. Calcutta: CMDA, 1974. Mimeo.

―――. *The Pavement-Dwellers of Calcutta.* Paper prepared for the UN Centre for Housing, Building and Planning, 1977. Calcutta: CMDA, n.d. Mimeo.

―――. *Typology of Slum and Squatter Settlements in the Metropolis.* Addendum to *The Pavement-Dwellers of Calcutta.* Calcutta: CMDA, n.d. Mimeo.

―――. *Shelter for the Poor in Calcutta: The Myth and the Reality.* Paper prepared for a Workshop on Homes for the Homeless. Calcutta, December 1986.

―――. *Land, Finance and Planning: Have the Parameters Gone Haywire?* Paper presented at the World Congress of Human Settlements in Developing Countries. New Delhi, December 1988.

Mukherjee, Sudhendu, and Andrea Menefee Singh. "Hierarchical and Symbiotic Relationships among the Urban Poor: A Report on Pavement Dwellers in Calcutta." In UNCHS (Habitat), *The Residential Circumstances of the Urban Poor in Developing Countries.* New York: Praeger, 1981.

Mumford, Lewis. *The City in History.* New York: Harcourt Brace, 1961.

Nair, P. Thankappan. *Calcutta in the 18th Century.* Calcutta: Firma KLM, 1984.

―――. *A History of Calcutta's Streets.* Calcutta: Firma KLM, 1987.

―――. *Calcutta in the 19th Century (Company's Days).* Calcutta: Firma KLM, 1989.

NIUA (National Institute of Urban Affairs). *Structure and Performance of Informal Enterprises: A Study of Four Cities.* NIUA Research studies series no. 19. New Delhi: NIUA, 1988.

Pakrasi, Kanti B. "Occupation, Class, Migration, and Family Structure among the Refugees of West Bengal, 1947–48." *Man in India,* 47, no. 3 (1967), pp. 200–213.

―――. *The Uprooted: A Sociological Study of the Refugees of West Bengal, India.* Calcutta: Editions Indian, 1971.

Racine, Jean, ed. *Calcutta 1981: The City, Its Crisis and the Debate on Urban Planning and Development.* New Delhi: Concept, 1990.

Ray, N.K. *A Short History of Calcutta, Town and Suburbs.* 1901. Reprint, Calcutta: Raddhi-India, 1982.

Ray, Nisitha Ranjana. *Calcutta: The Profile of a City.* Calcutta: K.P. Bagchi, 1986.

Ray, Pranabranjan. "Urbanization in Colonial Situation: Serampore." In *Trends in Socio-Economic Change in India, 1871–1961.* Simla: Indian Institute of Advanced Study, 1969.

Ray, Rajat. *Urban Roots of Indian Nationalism: Pressure Groups and Conflicts of Interest in Calcutta City Politics, 1875–1939.* New Delhi: Vikas, 1979.

Ray, S.B. "A Massive Attack on Bustees." In Indian Chamber of Commerce, *Toward a Better Calcutta.* Calcutta: 1965.

Row, Arthur T. *An Evaluation of the Calcutta Planning and Development Project 1961–1974.* Report for the Ford Foundation. New Delhi, October 1974.

Roy, Biren. *Calcutta, 1481–1981: Marshes to Metropolis.* Calcutta: National Council of Education, 1982.

Roy, Dilip K. "The Supply of Land for the Slums of Calcutta." In S. Angel, R.W. Archer, S. Tanphiphal, and E.A. Wegelin, eds., *Land for Housing the Poor.* Singapore: Select Books, 1983.

Roy, N.R. *City of Job Charnock.* Calcutta: Victoria Memorial, 1979.

Roy, Prabuddha Nath. "Calcutta: The Myth of Decay." In Government of West Bengal, *Calcutta's Urban Future.* Calcutta: 1991.

Roy, Prodipto. "Urbanization of Slum Improvement: A Middle Range Theory." In Council for Social Development and Ramakrishna Mission, *Symposium on Urbanization and Slums,* Delhi, April 26–28, 1993.

Roy, Ranajit. *The Agony of West Bengal.* Calcutta: New Age, 1972.

Roy, Sanjay K. "Life in Calcutta Slums." In Council for Social Development and Ramakrishna Mission, *Symposium on Urbanization and Slums,* April 26–28, 1993.

Roy, Subhankar. "The Kansa Baniks of Simla Para, Calcutta." M.S. unpublished thesis, University of Calcutta, 1982.

Sales and Display Publications, Seminar on Calcutta and Its Problems, *Calcutta Today: A Comprehensive Survey,* Calcutta: Rupa, 1970.

Samaddar, Sivaprasad. *Calcutta Is.* Calcutta: Calcutta Corporation, 1978.

Sarkar, Tanika. *Bengal, 1928–1934: The Politics of Protest.* Delhi and New York: Oxford University Press, 1987.

Sarma, Jyotirmoyee. *Caste Dynamics among the Bengali Hindus.* Calcutta: Firma KLM, 1980.

———. "Residence in Ownership Flats in Calcutta." *Man in India,* 69, no. 2 (1989), pp. 114–158.

Sanyal, Biswapriya, and Meenu Tewar. *Politics and Institutions in Urban Development: The Story of the CMDA.* Draft report for the World Bank, March 1990.

Sanyal, Hitesranjan. *Social Mobility in Bengal.* Calcutta: Papyrus, 1981.

Sen, Asok. *The Bindery Workers of Daftaripara.* Occasional paper 127. Calcutta: Center for Studies in Social Sciences, April 1991.

———. *Life and Labour in a Squatter Colony.* Occasional paper 138. Calcutta: Center for Studies in Social Sciences, October 1992.

Sen, Asok, and Alok Banerjee. *Migrants in the Calcutta Metropolitan District.* Occasional paper 62. Calcutta: Center for Studies in Social Sciences, 1983.

Sen, Jai. *The Unintended City: An Essay on the City of the Poor.* Calcutta: Unnayan, 1978.

———. Series of articles on "marginal land settlements" in *Amrita Bazar Patrika,* July 1986.

Sen, Saurendra Nath. *The City of Calcutta: A Socio-Economic Survey, 1954–55 to 1957–58.* Calcutta: Bookland, 1960.

Siddiqui, M.K.A. "The Neighbourhood in Calcutta." In Siddiqui, ed., *Aspects of Society and Culture in Calcutta.* Calcutta: Anthropological Survey of India, Government of India, 1982.

Siddiqui, M.K.A., and Pranab Jyoti De. "The Image-Makers of Kumartoli." In Siddiqui, ed., *Aspects of Society and Culture in Calcutta.* Calcutta: Anthropological Survey of India, Government of India, 1982.

Siddiqui, M.K.A., and S.P. Lala. "The Darzis of Metiaburj." In Siddiqui, ed. *Aspects of Society and Culture in Calcutta.* Calcutta: Anthropological Survey of India, Government of India, 1982.

Singh, A.J.B. "Under Cover of the Night," *Telegraph* (Calcutta), July 25, 1993.

Singh, Raghubir, and Joseph Lelyveld. *Calcutta.* Hong Kong: Perennial Press, 1975.

Sinha, Dixshit. "Life in a Calcutta Slum," In Surajit Sinha, ed., *Cultural Profile of Calcutta.* Calcutta: Indian Anthropological Society, 1972.

Sinha, Narendra K. *The History of Bengal: 1757–1905.* Berkeley and Los Angeles: University of California Press, 1967.

Sinha, Pradip. *Calcutta in Urban History.* Calcutta: Berkeley and Los Angeles: University of California Press, 1978.

———. "Genesis of a Colonial City." In *Calcutta's Urban Future.* Calcutta: Government of West Bengal, 1991.

Sinha, Surajit. "Scope for Urban Anthropology and the City of Calcutta." *Indian Anthropological Society,* 5, nos. 1–2 (April–October 1970), pp. 65–78.

———. ed. *Cultural Profile of Calcutta.* Calcutta: Indian Anthropological Society, 1972.

Sinha, Swapan Kumar. *Child Labour in Calcutta.* Calcutta: Naya Prokah, 1991.

Sivaramakrishnan, K.C. "Slum Improvement in Calcutta." *Assignment Children,* 40 (October/December 1977), pp. 87–115.

———. "The Slum Improvement Programme in Calcutta: The Role of CMDA." In Alfred de Souze, ed., *The Indian City: Poverty, Ecology and Urban Development.* New Delhi: South Asia Books, 1977.

Sivaramakrishnan, K.C., and Leslie Green. *Metropolitan Management: The Asian Experience.* New York: Oxford University Press, 1986.

Theroux, Paul. *The Great Railway Bazaar.* New York: Washington Square Press, 1985.

Turner, Roy, ed. *India's Urban Future.* Berkeley and Los Angeles: University of California Press, 1962.

UN (United Nations). *Population Growth and Policies in Mega-Cities: Calcutta.* New York: United Nations, 1986.

UNESCO (United Nations Educational, Scientific, and Cultural Organization). "Social Aspects of Small Industries in India." In *Studies in Howrah and Bombay of Selected Turning Shops, Blacksmithies, and Art Silk Units.* New Delhi: Research Centre on Social and Economic Development in Southern Asia, 1962.

Unnayan (Progress). *Basti Movement in Calcutta: Housing Struggle of Basti Dwellers in the 1950's in Calcutta.* Howrah: Offset Process, n.d.

———. *Rickshaws in Calcutta.* Calcutta: Unnayan, February 1981.

———. *Towards Planning for the Real Calcutta.* Paper prepared for a CMDA seminar, February 16–17, 1983. Calcutta: Unnayan, n.d. Mimeo.

World Bank. *Project Performance Audit Report: India First Calcutta Urban Development Project.* Washington, D.C.: World Bank, June 30, 1982. Mimeo.

————. *Project Completion Report: India Second Calcutta Urban Development Project.* Washington, D.C.: World Bank, October 16, 1987. Mimeo.

————. *Project Appraisal Report: India Third Calcutta Urban Development Project.* Washington, D.C.: World Bank. Mimeo. (See especially Municipal Development Program and Small-Scale Enterprise Program.)

————. *Project Completion Report: India Third Calcutta Urban Development Project.* Washington, D.C.: World Bank, June 30, 1993. Mimeo.

Index

Frederic C. Thomas received a B.A. in international relations from Harvard College in 1952, studied Arabic under a Fullbright scholarship in Cairo, and in 1956 obtained a Ph.D. in Anthropology from the University of London.

His subsequent career has been devoted to Third World development: with the Peace Corps (1961–67) as country director in Morocco and subsequently on Somalia; with the U.S. Agency for International Development (1967–73) as coordinator for food aid in Jordan and among Palestinian refugees, and as focal point for relief assistance in newly independent Bangladesh; with the United Nations Development Program (1973–88) as deputy resident representative in Saudi Arabia and later as resident representative in Haiti responsible for coordinating all UN technical assistance; as an independent consultant on Third World development issues (1989-present) undertaking assignments on behalf of the UN and U.S. government and voluntary agencies to evaluate development projects in Asia. He has conducted research in Calcutta intermittently over the past ten years, focusing on slum improvements, the impact of poverty on ethnic and occupational groups, and the vitality of the informal sector.

He is presently a research scholar at the Center for South Asian Studies of the University of California, Berkeley.